MAD MORGAN
Child of the Forest, Man of the Mines

the autobiography of

Reginald Victor Morgan

as told to his daughter

Elaine Morgan

Best Wishes

Reg & Elaine Morgan

Pavan Press

Illustrations by Elaine Morgan

Published by Pavan Press
1 Carrbottom Avenue, Bradford BD5 9BE
01274 573104

Editors Frances McNeil and Alan Pascoe

Set in Times New Roman 10 pt

Printed by BM Printers, Huddersfield

ISBN 0 9525547 0 4

In Memory of my dear Mother, Kate Amelia,
and my beloved Wife, Phyllis

FOREWORD

It is with immense honour that I write the Foreword to this work. The book is about one person's passage through life, not someone who has amassed both fame and fortune but one whose struggle makes compelling reading.

The story begins before the First World War, in the industrial whirlpool of South Wales at Cefn Fforest, in the area known then as Bedwellty. There is a short, idyllic childhood in the mining Town of Cinderford in the Forest of Dean, a working life in the mines and retirement in a South Wales Mining Valley at Hengoed, Glamorgan.

It takes courage to survive through economic depression, world war and bitter strikes, through hardships that most people cannot even begin to contemplate.

Reginald Victor Morgan is known amongst butties as Mad Morgan - a title he earned for his daredevil dispatch riding in the Second World War. To me he is more affectionately known as Uncle Reg: Soldier, Welsh Miner and Rebel, but above all a Forester.

This man, without knowing, shaped my own beliefs. He has been my mentor, a strong character and a staunch advocate of social justice and fairness for working people.

With great pride and passion, I recommend his story to you. I am sure it will raise the reader's awareness, and no doubt for some it will raise a tear.

Graham Leslie Morgan
Mayor of Cinderford
Forest of Dean
Gloucestershire
April, 1995

The Right Honourable The Viscount Tonypandy PC, DCL

House of Lords

As time rolls on, the circle of those of us who retain vivid memories of life in South Wales during the inter-war years, grows smaller & smaller.

This lively story of just one of the miners, adds an authentic account to the revolutionary changes that have taken place this century.

Change rarely takes place by accident; in our Parliamentary democracy, change comes through the sheer guts & determination of ordinary people, to use the House of Commons as a doorway to a better quality of life.

'Mad Morgan' typifies the strength of workers in the 1920's, 1930's, & the 1940's.

I commend it warmly,

George Tonypandy

1 - *Born in Monmouthshire*

It was by a twist of fate that I was born in South Wales. Both my mother and my father were of mining families but originally from Cinderford, which at that time was regarded as the Capital of the Royal Forest of Dean. My birth, on 16th April, 1911, was a home confinement in my grandmother's two up, two down terrace house in the Parish of Bedwellty, in the County of Monmouthshire (now Gwent) and to this day it amazes me to think that my grandmother reared fourteen children in that tiny house. My mother was one of those fourteen. My parents' reason for being in Wales is easy to explain - employment!

Jobs were hard to find in the years before the First World War, with little employment available in the Forest. My father and maternal grandfather decided to look for work in Wales and as there were no cars or buses in those days, they had to use, as the saying goes, `Shanks' pony'. They foot slogged from Cinderford to South Wales, a distance of 52 miles or more, following a meandering course of woodland, hills, mountains and rivers - the `Sylvan Wye' of Wordsworth fame. Being men who liked their drink, the pubs along the way gave them all the sustenance they required and the river provided cool comfort for the blisters on their feet. How they got their hobnail boots back on, I can only guess.

On arrival, they managed to find work in the local coal levels, not at that time the deep coal mines of South Wales. These levels were near the surface and fresh air, though it was still hard graft and the pay a mere pittance. Yet for men with wives and children to support it was better than nothing at all. There were no `hand outs' in those days. People had to sell what decent furniture they had before the Parish would even consider giving support and even then you were damn lucky if you got anything. If you did not work you did not eat, it was as simple as that. Everybody was in the same boat and as a result we were a very close-knit community.

Life was a real drudgery for the women, trying to make ends meet to feed their families. Many died young or were old before their time. Women were regarded as chattel, to fetch, carry, sweat and slave, to bear many children and work miracles to feed their master and offspring. The women were saints and somehow managed to cope. The poor always seemed to have large families. Many children suffered and died in infancy, from malnutrition, consumption, rheumatic fever or common illnesses which are cured so easily now. The situation was similar to that found today in many South American and African countries. Poverty breeds suffering. You are either very poor or very rich. As it says in the New Testament, `The poor are always with us'.

My mother and grandmother were two of those remarkable women. Gran was very tiny yet against all the odds most of the fourteen children she gave birth to survived. She was indeed a miracle worker.

I liked my gran with her fairy tales, stories of the Forest of Dean. I loved to listen even to the scary ones.

Granddad Morgan was a good worker, but a hard drinker. Even so, he never attempted to strike Gran. Drink, gambling, horses and cards were his vices and he hated losing at anything. He would very often come home at night in a drunken stupor and collapse in the hall. Gran used to leave him there. Yet come morning he would be up and out to work as if nothing untoward had happened. He was very tall and as a result of an accident in the level, where a piece of steel penetrated his eye causing him to lose it, he wore a patch over his eye. His great passion was his garden and chickens, a welcome supplement to the family diet. I remember all the pictures of cockerels which decorated the kitchen walls - such beautiful, colourful birds. I used to look at them for hours, fascinated by the shades and hues of Rhode Island Reds, Leghorns, Bantams, Indian Game and others.

Although very young, I remember one particular saying of Granddad's, uttered when two of my uncles were about to get married.

"You think that you are marrying little goldfinches, but they could turn out to be water-wagtails. Well, Harry, Jimmy, you make your bed and you lie on it. No good coming to me for help."

Oddly enough, that is how it turned out for both of them. Their wives were `wagtails'.

My father, who worked in the same coal level as Granddad, was a very hard drinker. This was to have a devastating effect on my mother's and my life. He was a true Victorian, a hard taskmaster and I, being the first-born, took the brunt of his anger if things went wrong. My mother, Kate, would do her best to defend me and sometimes both of us suffered as a result. Drink was his demon and he was demonic in his drink. He used to beat me with a leather strap, buckle and all. At an early age I learned to be afraid of him. He never showed me any affection. Yet he was a smart man, about five foot five in height, with a moustache. He always wore a trilby. Street angel, kitchen devil - a real Jekyll and Hyde. My mother, God bless her, was my comfort and her love made my life worthwhile.

Mam was petite, like Gran, dark haired and good looking. She took great pride in her dress and she was a marvellously talented seamstress. Many old clothes were altered and converted into decent looking blouses and skirts for herself and trousers and tops for me. She would take the best parts of worn out clothes and make up little suits for me that looked like new as there was no money available for such luxuries as brand new clothes. Even our shoes were patched with leather from old boots that had been thrown away. Mam was my whole world and I loved her dearly. My lullabies, when she was able to find the time to nurse and comfort me, were hymns, especially her favourite *Abide With Me*. She worked from dawn until dusk to make ends meet. Oh how she must have worried inwardly, poor dear Mam. God bless her!

One of my earliest memories was at the age of three, a very tragic one not connected with the family. I happened to be out in the street when a man came running down the road.

"Terrible news, a pit has blown up in the next valley. Hundreds dead," he shouted.

The explosion at Senghenydd Colliery, near Caerphilly, Mid Glamorgan on 14th October, 1913 turned out to be one of the worst mine disasters in this country. Nearly every house in the village of Senghenydd lost loved ones. Some lost two or three from the same household. Fathers, brothers, uncles, sons, nephews, from boys on the threshold of life to grandfathers in the autumn of their lives. John H. Brown has written of the tragedy in *The Valley of the Shadow*. Four hundred and thirty nine men and boys perished in the gas explosion and a rescuer was killed the following day. Umpteen pit ponies also died. Unless you have worked in the mines it is difficult to comprehend the dangers faced by those brave and courageous men. Such tragedies affect not only the village concerned but mining communities everywhere.

Their tragedy was ours.

The following year, the War to end all wars broke out, World War I. My mother's sister Sophia lived in a street parallel to ours and was married to Uncle Jack Little whose family came from Stourbridge. Two of his nephews worked in the famous Stuart Crystal Company. One was a glass blower and the other was a glass engraver.

Uncle Jack's father was responsible for keeping the furnace going for the production of glass-making. My mother had a beautiful set of glass crystal bells from the factory and really cherished them. Uncle Jack fought at the Battle of Ypres, October to November 1914. He was an artificer. Under fire, he managed to save his guns from being captured. For his gallantry, he was awarded the Military Medal and we were very proud of him. I remember my aunty recalling Uncle Jack's remark, "By the time the church bells in England were ringing, celebrating the capture of Ypres, the British Army had lost it again".

At three and a half, I started school at Fairview Infants School, now alas demolished. The school was not too far away from my grandmother's house and within easy walking distance for my mother and me. It was pretty safe to walk along the roads then, with no traffic problems. From the main road, there was a dirt track leading towards the school, with a small pond and brook nearby. In Spring you would see frog spawn which was a great attraction for the school children. Like all children I was drawn to water - another worry for Mam. On the other side of the brook was a row of terrace houses, and a long black pipe protruding from a bank provided constant running spring water. Everybody obtained their drinking water from this source and it tasted beautiful. Cool and refreshing, real quality drinking water without pollution or the threat of it.

There was also a billy goat tethered on the grass, which the older boys teased unmercifully, knowing full well that it could not retaliate. Coming home from school with my friends one day, I was thirsty and went to drink from the pipe. The billy goat decided that we were the enemy and started to charge. Unfortunately, he was untethered and we had to run like the wind. My Aunty Poppit lived nearby and the goat chased us all the way down the hill to Aunty's front door. We did not have a chance to close the front door, but managed to shut the inner door. This was lucky for us but not so lucky for Aunty Poppit. The goat chewed up her best curtains and proceeded to devour them. He eventually decided he had had enough and found his own way out, to our great relief. We waited a while and then headed for home.

My stay at this school was short, because my father decided to return to the Royal Forest of Dean and his home at Cinderford. Our few possessions were packed and we said goodbye to Grandmother and Grandfather. I could not understand why they were not coming with us. They were a part of my family!

It was to be my first ride on a train, and a great adventure with the locomotive, huffing and puffing along the track. I looked at my mother for reassurance and never ventured from her side. The train sped down the valley with the Rhymney river on our right, passed mountains, through farming areas, and finally arrived at Newport, Gwent. From there we caught a train to Blakeney, leaving the mountains of Wales behind. We travelled through lovely countryside, with the River Severn as our constant companion. The train chugged along towards Chepstow, with the Castle on the hill and then proceeded to make its way to Lydney.

The Forest of Dean, our new home, lay ahead.

Whether it was the motion of the train or sheer exhaustion, I must have fallen asleep. After all, it was my first great exploration into the big wide world and I was only a little chap of three years and eleven months. As my mother lifted me into her arms, I was aroused from my deep contented sleep to find that we were alighting from the train at Blakeney Station in the Forest of Dean.

2 - *Child of the Forest*

The short train ride from Blakeney to Cinderford took us through forest, where great trees touched the sky. I had never seen so many trees before, except the apple tree in my grandmother's garden and the Christmas tree. We came to a clearing in the forest, which I heard my father say was the Eastern United Mine. As we continued along the railway track, a mass of yellow blossom greeted our tired eyes. It was called Primrose Hill, and spring had arrived in the Forest!

From Ruspidge Station, we walked to a small house close to The Dog Inn. In later years, I learned that this house was built in the eighteenth century. It belonged to my grandfather, as did the Inn and six houses in Cinderford, plus a large piece of land. How could Grandfather be here? I left him and Gran! Mam explained that these grandparents were my father's parents. We were to stay with them until dad found a house. They welcomed us and gave us much appreciated refreshments. I settled down to sleep, my mind teeming with images of what I had seen.

Morning came and I awoke in a strange room with no sign of Mam or Dad. I became very frightened and began to cry for my mother. Mam was soon by my side comforting me. We went downstairs and Grandmother was making tea and toast for breakfast. Dad had already gone out in search of employment and Grandfather had gone to his work at the Cinderford to Blakeney railway. He was in charge of the whole railway line.

Grandmother was a thin, short lady, pleasant and kind and lovable as a grandmother should be. I now had two people fussing over me - Mam and Gran - which was reassuring. I knew I would like my new home in the Forest!

Dad came home and had found work at Light Moor Colliery, about one and a half miles from the house, easy walking distance. Three miles walking was nothing to people in those days, but it must have seemed like a hundred after working long hours in the mine all day.

After tea, Dad went out searching for a house to rent. Grandfather arrived home from work and settled down to his meal. He was about five foot seven in height, which seemed very tall to me at the time, and he had an authoritative air about him. He looked as if he would stand no nonsense. He was clean shaven and smartly dressed. He really cared about his appearance. I was a little afraid of him, answering yes or no to his questions as carefully as I could, but Mam and Gran were there to reassure me. Anyway, I think he liked me as far as I could tell. We were to remain at my grandparents' for several days, while Dad continued his search for a house. It was a little crowded when we were all home together, but we managed not to get under each other's feet. The grown-ups talked most of the evening and I was tucked up in bed early. Eventually, Dad managed to find a house at a reasonable rent.

Bags packed, we were quickly on the move again. The house was near the Nags Head pub and was a small two up, two down, with the added luxury of an indoor well with a cover. No taps, just a bucket to draw water for our needs. The windows were small, the ceilings low and the floors were flagstone and cold underfoot. There was very little furniture. There was a black-leaded grate and oven for cooking, plus the comfort of a warm coal fire in the hearth. A tiny staircase lead to the small, yet cosy looking bedrooms. The `earth' lavatory in the garden was a wooden seat with a hole in the middle, housed within cold stone walls and covered by a makeshift roof.

When we had settled in, Mam decided it was time I attended school again. Off we went, to St Whites School in Cinderford where I was handed over to the head teacher's care until school was over for the day. Mam said she would be there to take me home after school. Having been to school in South Wales, I was not afraid, but a little nervous of my new teacher and the children in my class. After all I was a stranger to them as they were strangers to me. The newness soon wore off and I settled in well with the other pupils. There was always the odd one out in every school and you can't be friends with everyone, but that did not worry me. I was a Morgan and could take care of myself.

In the school playground there were two `conker' trees, so the boys told me.

"What are conker trees?" I asked.

"You'll soon find out when the time comes," I was told. "We'll have a whale of a time."

I was really looking forward to that.

The lesson I enjoyed most were the nature walks with our teacher in the forest. She was making me aware of the sights, sounds and smells of the forest. Everything I saw fascinated me and I thought that I was in wonderland. Squirrels ran across my path and scampered up trees, rabbits scurried away, pheasants startled me as they took fright and flew up in front of me. If I was very quiet, I might see a deer in the deep, dark, dank woods. Occasionally, the silence of the forest was broken by the warbling of songbirds. It was very difficult to spot them because of all the foliage. The many broad leaf trees were ideal for songbirds. The fir trees were a haven for all kinds of creatures. There were wild flowers of every description. The teacher must have been exhausted by all my questions.

"What's this? What's that?"

The woodland dells were amass with millions of blue-bells whose scent filled the air. A sense of freedom engulfed my whole body and I was intoxicated by that magical place!

To think I was actually living here in the Forest of Dean. What a wonderful playground! We did not venture too far from the teacher. Every forest path looked identical, and all with sheep grazing. You could very easily get lost. Then the ghosts of the Forest would get you. Oh yes, there were ghosts, according to my grandmother. The lesson over, I hurried home to tell Mam about all the exciting things I had seen in the forest that day.

Mam would prepare dinner, timed for when Dad finished work at the mine and she would ensure that food was on the table as Dad walked through the door. She knew this was what he expected. While Dad washed and changed his clothes to go out, Mam would sometimes take me over to Grandfather's with the dirty washing, which I would help to carry. I was more of a hindrance than a help, dropping items on the ground as we walked. Mam never complained, just smiled and told me to pick them up.

At Grandfather's house, there was a communal wash house for the tenants. Inside was a large black water-filled caldron above a blazing fire. The other part of the wash house, separated by a brick wall, housed a communal oven for baking bread. Tenants would alternate the days for washing and baking bread. There's nothing like the aroma of freshly baked bread, but imagine the smell of washing clashing with the smell of baking.

While Mam and Grandmother got on with the washing, I would slip away to watch Grandfather working in his vegetable garden, his pride and joy. He grew cabbages, carrots, onions and potatoes which were part of our staple diet. Money was in short supply and you had to improvise as best you could. He also kept geese and pigs, so we were never short of bacon and ham. When Grandfather invited me to feed the geese I shied away. I was happier on the other side of the fence. One particular goose took an instant dislike to me and the feeling was mutual! I used to watch the geese as they waddled up the hill, took off and flew to the pond on the other side of the road. In the late evening they would waddle back up the hill to settle down for the night.

My Grandmother's brother was also a keen gardener and used his wooden leg as a gardening tool. When he worked in the garden, he made a line with two sticks, to which a piece of string was attached. Then he would make a hole with his wooden leg and drop a potato in the hole, repeating this action along the line, row after row. A wheelwright, he made his wooden legs with a hollow section at the top where he stashed his money, sometimes a golden sovereign or two. He was a pleasant man and used to laugh a lot, exposing the few teeth he had. He was also a great bird fancier and had an outside aviary with canaries, budgerigars, finches and a few foreign birds. Birds were his great passion. I did not mind feeding them as they were more my size.

Washing days were the times when Mam, although busy, could relax and have a good chat with Grandmother and the neighbours. It was the one time that Mam did not have to keep her eye on me constantly. She knew I was in safe hands and had plenty to occupy my mind. I enjoyed our regular visits to Grandfather's. For me it was playtime, but not for Mam. In the evening, we trudged home with the washing. There was always tomorrow to look forward to.

3 - *Sundays & Special Days*

Sunday was my favourite day, especially if the weather was good. Sometimes in the afternoon, to my delight, Mam would take me for a walk to Littledean, to visit my aunts who had a small-holding with a duck pond. From where we lived, it was uphill all the way to Littledean but there was no rush and we took our time, enjoying the sunshine and pure fresh forest air. From the summit of the hill we had a magnificent view of the River Severn which looked like a silver snake slithering its way along the valley. On a clear day, we could see Gloucester Cathedral, where the martyred Edward II is buried. We passed an eerie, partly ruined house which Mam said was the Old Grange. Apparently my grandmother in South Wales, a Forester herself, lived there as a young girl. Her family were the last inhabitants of the Old Grange, which was originally a gentleman's residence with a garden and beautiful stone statues.

The City of Bristol was formerly famous, or infamous, for its slave trade and the owner of Old Grange had purchased several slaves. One of these slaves, unhappy with his fate, murdered his master. The room in which the murder took place was permanently locked in Grandmother's time and no one dared enter.

My grandfather courted my grandmother when she lived there. One day he decided to take a short cut down a lane leading to the Grange. As he did so, he heard a crash in the hedge and felt a strong rush of air. It shook him for a while but, being a man without fears, he quickly recovered. It was not his imagination because others who passed that way had strange experiences too. This was truly one of the ghost stories of the Forest, still remembered to this day.

Of course there is nothing of the Old Grange left today, except an odd stone or two hidden beneath the undergrowth. The mist still hovers around the site - that hasn't changed.

Mam and I would spend a pleasant hour or two with my aunts, or Mam's close friend who lived in that area. They would fuss over me, offering a biscuit or a piece of cake and a drink. Mam was reluctant to accept their offers because Dad had a very strict ruling on the subject.

He would say, "People have enough to do to feed themselves, without feeding others."

But they insisted and Mam graciously accepted as she did not wish to offend. However, it was never mentioned at home.

Visiting time over and farewells said, Mam and I would set out on the return journey. Preparations must be made for the start of another working week on Monday morning. Work for Dad, school for me.

One day after school, Mam was there to collect me as usual, but a stranger dressed in sailor's uniform accompanied her. Mam's brother, Uncle Seymour, was on leave and had decided to pay us a short visit. It was clear Mam was pleased to see him. He gave me a piggy-back ride all the way home. As Mam prepared dinner, they talked about the War and other things that were over my head. Mam mentioned something about a baby. Over dinner the adult chatter continued until out of the blue Uncle Seymour asked Mam if he could take me to the cinema.

What was a cinema? I was soon to find out.

Dad said it was alright, so off we went. I cannot remember the film, but I must have enjoyed it.

Mam always found time for me no matter what she was doing and on this particular day she told me that I was going to have a baby brother or sister.

"Will the baby come for my birthday?" I asked.

"No," she replied. "It will be here at the end of June."

I was disappointed but at least I would have someone to play with when the baby came.

Birthdays then were very simple affairs because the money was just not around. Mam always did the best she could and there was a cake for tea, a card and a present. Usually it was clothing that Mam had made for me. I was really chuffed when I told people that my mother had made something especially for my birthday.

As a birthday treat, Mam would take me to see Grandmother's nephew, Sim Dyer. He had a team of eight enormous shire horses. A timber haulier by trade, Sim was involved in forestry work, cutting down tall oak trees and hauling the trunks from Cinderford to the saw mills in Gloucester - a distance of approximately twelve miles. It must have been very difficult negotiating the downhill sections along the route with the weight of several oak trunks behind and the team in front. The wooden brakes were stretched to their limits. They were applied so heavily that they began to smoke with friction and water had to be poured over the brakes to prevent them catching fire. Sim had a terrible accident when an anchor chain slipped and one of the oak trunks moved and crushed his arm. It had to be amputated to the elbow. Yet he survived this and continued his forestry work, controlling eight horses with one arm.

Sometimes Uncle Will would offer to take me for a ride in his pony and trap. Mam was not too keen on the idea because Uncle Will liked a pint or two and very often these jaunts would end up outside his favourite watering holes.

"Just a short trip, Will," Mam would say.

I thoroughly enjoyed my rides, not realising why Mam was concerned and so relieved when I came home safe and sound. The pony and trap were Uncle Will's pride and joy and he took good care of both. The stable was of a better standard than some housing of the time. It was like a small bungalow, spotlessly clean and warm, with water laid on. Uncle Will certainly knew how to care for his pony.

My pals at school would have liked a ride in the pony and trap but I did not like to ask Uncle Will. Anyway, there was something far more exciting on the agenda. The whole village was buzzing with excitement. A travelling fair had arrived in Cinderford and set up camp at the station. My pals at school couldn't concentrate on their lessons and I wondered what all the fuss was about.

Mam confirmed that a fair had arrived but was too busy to tell me about it.

"Later," she said.

And later, when Dad had eaten, washed and changed and gone to his local and Mam was quietly sewing and mending, I decided to go and look for the fair.

The music was my guide. I followed its sound.

People with children were milling around red and white striped tents. On tables were ornaments, dolls and trinkets. Children were throwing hoops to try and win a prize. At another table, you paid your money and pulled a string to get a present. Some men were shooting at clay pipes with a gun to win yet another prize. The music got louder and the main attraction came into view. It was the horses roundabout which the boys had talked about in school. The large, multi-coloured horses bobbed up and down, down and up as the roundabout spun at an increasing speed, encircled by lights. Riders held tight to each horse's pole. Nearby was a dirty, noisy machine which I later learned was a traction engine. I looked around and saw people eating pink fluffy stuff on sticks.

I don't know how long I wandered about in astonished amazement before I realised I was lost. Fortunately I had a lot of relatives in Cinderford.

I heard my grandfather's niece say, "I'm sure that's Kate's boy."

They took me to their home, gave me food and put me to bed. My Mam, searching for me, having guessed I had wandered to the fair, met Grandfather's niece, on her way to tell Mam that I was safe.

"He'll be alright, Kate. He's tucked up in bed. Leave him until morning," she said.

Mam, however, knew that Dad would be very angry. She took me home and put me straight to bed before Dad got back.

The following morning after Dad had gone to work, Mam told me I had done a very naughty thing and I must not do anything like that again. Most of all I must never mention it to Dad because he would give me a hiding.

Apart from our evening meal, I saw very little of my father during the week. He was either at work or out at the pub. At the weekend he would be working in the garden, or he would go into the forest to collect wood for the fire for the following week.

He was always too busy to find time for me.

Miners had little time off and just seven holidays a year: two at Christmas, two at Easter, one on May Day and two at August Bank Holiday.

May Day, Mam explained, was to celebrate the beginning of summer. The miners and tradespeople donated sums of money for this day as a special treat for all the children and adults. The Mayor of Cinderford would officiate over the entire proceedings. There would be a big parade with jazz bands leading the procession through Cinderford. Horse drawn floats competing for Best Float Prize carried excited children in fancy dress. I wanted so much to go on a float, but Mam said I was too young. The last float carried the May Queen and her attendants, selected from the local girls of the village. The Mayor would officially crown the Queen of the May and celebrations would begin.

Rain or shine, people were determined to enjoy the day. First came athletics with races of every kind. Two legged races, three legged races, combined efforts of fathers and sons against rival fathers and sons. Sack races where most competitors fell before reaching the finishing line. Pancake races where most pancakes ended not in the mouth but on the ground, and the egg and spoon races which left a real mess.

Win or lose, everybody was a winner that day.

It was thirsty work and most of the dads slipped away to the beer tent whilst the mothers took their refreshment at the tea and cake tent. Everybody was laughing and having a great time, apart from the odd child getting a clip around the ear for some misdemeanour arising from over-excitement. After all, these special days were few and far between!

I did not want the day to end and I think everyone felt the same. It was a perfect day and the weather was kind.

"Goodnight Kate, goodnight Sam, see you in the morning," people shouted.

I went to bed that night a very happy and contented child.

4 - *Summer & A Sister*

Summer was the loveliest time of year for me and when the sun shone it was difficult to concentrate on lessons. I would sometimes gaze out of the window and daydream, being brought back to earth with a bump.

"Reg Morgan. Get on with your work."

In the evening when Mam was not too busy she would take me for walks in the forest. It was a wonderful place for a child to grow up, mysterious and magical. Sometimes I would be St George slaying the Dragon, or Robin Hood in Sherwood Forest outwitting the Sheriff of Nottingham, or even King Arthur.

This is where I wanted to remain forever.

My jaunts into the forest with Mam grew less because Mam was becoming tired. She spent more time knitting and sewing tiny clothes for the baby.

"When will the baby come Mam?" I would say.

"Soon Reg, very soon," she replied.

Gran's brother, Mr Furlow, called one day carrying a wooden rocking cradle he had made. Mam was delighted. You could rock it to and fro with your foot as you sat in a chair knitting or sewing.

"Where do babies come from Mam?" I asked.

"From under the gooseberry bush," was her reply.

I never found any babies under gooseberry bushes.

Every morning I would wake with anticipation that the baby had finally arrived. But my elation was short lived.

"Not today love," Mam would say.

I would trudge along to school with a look of disappointment on my face. My pals did not bother to ask as my face betrayed everything. The teacher assured me that the baby would come and asked whether I wanted a brother or sister. I hadn't thought of that.

"A brother's best. A sister's a pest," one lad told me.

I wouldn't know as I had never had either before.

There were lots of things to learn at school. The three R's occupied my mind for most of the time but the days dragged as I waited and longed to have someone to play with at home.

On 20th June, 1915 my long-awaited sister Edytha finally came into the world. Of course I missed the big event because I was in school. When I arrived home there were several ladies busy in the tiny kitchen chatting excitedly and gulping tea. Grandmother did not notice me. I could not see Mam anywhere and pulled Grandmother's apron.

"Where's Mam?"

"Reg!" she exclaimed, "Your mother and baby sister are alright."

I could not believe it at first. A baby sister. At last I would have someone to play with.

"Can I see Mam and the baby?"

"Later. Come and have your tea first. Your Mam and the baby are sleeping at present."

I was desperate to see them. Although I was still only four years old I had waited so long for this great event. But Grandmother was adamant. It was agony having to wait until after tea. I scoffed it down as quickly as I could, much to Grandmother's disapproval. Finally, my grandmother took me aside and told me to pick a bunch of flowers.

There I was, flowers in hand as I climbed the stone stairs leading to the bedrooms. I knocked quietly and entered. Mam was lying in bed and looked pale and tired. In her arms she held a very small bundle wrapped in a shawl. As I approached Mam I held out the flowers. She smiled and asked me if I would like to see my sister. Mam unwrapped the shawl and there she was, a tiny mite the size of a doll. Much too small to play with. She was beautiful. She had a wisp of dark brown hair, the same colour as Mam's.

"Can I hold the baby's hand, Mam?" I asked.

"Of course you can," Mam replied.

It was the biggest thrill of my life. Such tiny fingers that seemed to cling to my own fingers as I held her hand.

"Was I as small as that, Mam?"

"Yes dear," Mam replied. "Be a good boy and put the flowers in water for me."

I wanted to stay with Mam and my baby sister of whom I was very proud but I went downstairs and did as Mam asked.

My father arrived home from the mine and washed and changed before dinner, which was unusual. I was bursting to tell someone.

"Dad, Dad, I have a baby sister. She's lovely. Can I have some water for the flowers, please."

My father filled the vase and said that he would take it up himself. I was a little disappointed because Mam had asked me to do it. I was determined to follow my father upstairs.

"It's your father's turn now, Reg, you can go up later," Gran said, her hand on my shoulder.

Too excited to play, I decided to break the great news to my neighbours. Of course most of them knew but feigned surprise. I wanted to see Mam and the baby again before I went to bed at 7 o'clock, so home I went. My father was getting ready to go out to his local to celebrate the birth of the baby and Grandmother remained to look after Mam, the baby and me.

Bedtime was fast approaching and after a thorough wash, including my ears, Grandmother gave me some warm milk and took me upstairs. We entered Mam's room as quietly as possible in case the baby was asleep. Mam was resting but still awake. She gave me a goodnight kiss.

"Goodnight love. Sleep tight and say your prayers," Mam said.

We left the room as quietly as we entered, glancing back at Mam as we closed the door. Grandmother tucked me into bed and left. Sleep did not come easy that night. I was too excited to settle down. I wished it was morning. I was desperately eager to tell my exciting news to everyone at school.

The next morning I went into Mam's bedroom. Mam was awake but the baby was sleeping so I gave Mam a kiss, peeped at my sister and went quietly out of the room and off to school, fit to burst with pride.

"Guess what! I have a baby sister," I shouted to my friends.

But they were more interested in the games they were playing and by the end of the day I had chattered on so much that my friends completely lost interest in me. My teacher was pleased though.

It was several days before Mam was up and about. Gradually things returned to normal. But now my sister demanded all the attention. We watched over her constantly as she slept or cried. Bath times were the worst as she did not like water. When Mam was busy she would let me rock the baby in the cradle. I enjoyed that. A little jealousy crept in as I felt my sister was getting all the attention. Mam realised this and would give me a hug and little tasks to do which she said were a great help to her. This made me feel important. Some evenings we would sit by the fire, I watching the different shapes conjured up by the flickering flames, Mam nursing the baby and singing her favourite hymns and lullabies, *The Day Thou Gavest* and *Cwm Rhondda (Bread of Heaven* or *Guide Me Oh Thy Great Jehovah*). It felt cosy and comforting. Mam had a sweet and gentle voice and I loved to hear her sing.

For most of the days that followed I was fully occupied between school, helping Mam around the house and keeping a protective eye on my baby sister who was now approaching five weeks old. I wouldn't even let the wind blow on her and was always close by when visitors approached her lying so vulnerable in the cradle.

Mam's flower garden, tiny as it was, looked pretty in summer, attracting bees and butterflies.

Our neighbours' fruit trees, especially the Victoria plum trees, were so heavily laden that the branches threatened to break. Supports were needed to prop up the branches from the sheer weight of the fruit. Wasps were everywhere. I soon learned to avoid them and guarded my sister when she was in her cradle in the garden.

The pears and apples were forming nicely on the trees but were not yet ready for picking. Dad's vegetable garden was looking neat and tidy with row upon row of vegetables like soldiers on parade. My favourite vegetables were new potatoes straight from the garden for Sunday dinner. Mam had no problem getting me to eat my greens.

Towards the end of July the Speech House Annual Gala took place. This weekend event was arranged by Miners for the benefit of the children. The Speech House, now a licensed hotel, represents the centre of the Forest. It was the hunting lodge of the kings and queens of England, hence the title Royal Forest of Dean. Around the Speech House many great oaks were planted by royalty, including one planted by Elizabeth I. It represented the Court of Law for the area where many a criminal awaited sentence. It is said that within its walls was once a suit of armour which belonged to Edward, the Black Prince of Crecy, famous to the English, infamous to the French for the notorious massacre in Limoges. He was buried at Canterbury Cathedral. The Forest was no longer the hunting ground of Kings but the happy hunting ground of children.

Villagers walked from miles around to attend this memorable event. There were races, games of hide and seek amongst the trees, picnics with sandwiches and cakes and the fly-swatter in hand. Old men smoked pipes and recalled the good old days. Fathers nipped off to the Speech House for refreshments leaving mothers chatting with friends whilst trying to keep an eye on excited children. One child always managed to get lost in the wood and there would be a general hue and cry and search parties organised by the men. The child's mother always got the blame, but it was the father's responsibility too. The day always ended happily. Eventually, it was time to round up waifs and strays and make our way home.

The baby was already asleep when we reached home. It was still light when I went to bed that evening. I found it difficult to sleep during the summer because of the light. I could not understand why I had to go to bed so early. But father was adamant. Seven o'clock it had to be.

5 - *Summer Scrapes & Autumn Mists*

Mam must have dreaded the summer holidays. When I was in school she knew exactly where I was. Now she had the burden of my being at home all day, getting up to mischief as boys naturally do when left to their own devices. Yet she managed to keep me busy for some part of the day helping around the house. I loved to help Mam and she never complained that I got under her feet. Sometimes we would go shopping in Cinderford, buying what little food we could afford.

There was always housework to be done and Mam relied on me to keep a careful eye on my baby sister whilst she got on with household chores. Mam took great pride in her rented home and it was spotlessly clean until my grubby little feet ploughed in through the door covered in mud from the brook. Poor Mam. She had enough to do looking after the baby and the home. Children are a great worry to their parents. I hope that I did not worry Mam too much.

There was one task Mam always hated yet it was an essential part of good housewifery: the weekly cleaning of the black lead grate. A woman was judged a good or bad housewife by the state of her grate. It was a hell of a task but once completed gave Mam great satisfaction. After lunch, Mam would let me go out to play with my friends in the village with the usual caution to be careful. Water was always a great attraction for my friends and me and we used to dare each other to jump across the brook. Sometimes I would succeed, other times I would land in the brook and get soaking wet. I knew I could not go home because if Dad found out I would get a hiding. Instead, my friends and I would go to the edge of the forest and hang our clothes on the branches of the trees, or lay them in the sun to dry.

Sometimes my friends and I went deeper into the forest without telling Mam. She worried because of the great number of disused open iron work shafts that pitted the area of Buckshaft and were very close to the surface. You could easily fall into them, especially if you were playing a game of Cowboys and Indians or hide and seek. After a while we became bored and decided that we would climb trees looking for birds nests, although by August most of the fledglings had flown. We did find some nests with the remains of baby birds or where eggs had failed to hatch. Inevitably one of us fell or tore clothes. The latter was worse because a bump or bruise could be hidden. Once I had a tear in my clothing, I knew I had to get home before my father. I would hurry home, carrying a bunch of wild flowers for my mother.

The flowers were not for appeasement because I had torn my clothes, but because I loved my mother dearly. That remains with me to this day.

Mam was forever mending my clothes and did her best to protect me from Dad's wrath whenever she could. At weekends it was a different matter. Dad was home from work and I had to be on my best behaviour. To avoid being around Dad I would wander over to Granddad's and help to gather potatoes as he dug them up. He would patiently tell me what to do and I would try to be useful. My grandfather had a better understanding of children than my father, even though he was very strict and proud.

Grandfather knew that life was no bed of roses for Mam and me.

The holidays came to an end. School felt like a cage to me. At least when a bird is released from its cage it's gone forever. But school was always there. The only things I liked were playtime, nature lessons and fights in the school yard.

It was Autumn, "Season of mists and mellow fruitfulness," as John Keats wrote. The apples were ripe for picking and some found their way into the pockets of school children. The older boys used to bully the younger into stealing apples and, if they refused, they would call them *chicken*. If I did something like that and my parents got wind of it, I knew what was waiting at home for me - a damned good hiding. I put up with the boys' taunts and teasing and refused. Not that I was an angel but the less trouble I got into, the fewer hidings I had. Anyway, there was always the windfall apples which owners allowed children to gather. Plus the added bonus of ripe juicy plums and pears.

At weekends Mam would ask me to gather blackberries to make a pie or tart for Sunday tea. Off I would go, bowl in one hand, stick in the other, to tackle brambles. Have you noticed that the biggest and best fruits are either too deep within the thicket or too high up to reach? Hence the stick. It proved a very useful tool. One blackberry for me, one for the bowl. My stomach held more blackberries than the bowl. Of course my tongue was a give-away.

Mam was good cook like most of her generation. Cooking was a real art and cooks had to know their fire heated ovens and how to bake different dishes according to the oven's temperature.

Autumn in the forest was the most beautiful season of the year. Gone were the luscious greens of summer and the golds and reds of autumn reigned supreme. There were acorns from the great oaks, chestnuts from the sweet chestnut trees and last but not least conkers from the horse chestnut trees. I had waited a long time for the conkers.

"What's the difference between a chestnut and a conker?" I asked.

"One you can eat, one is poison," was the reply.

The first rule was to find a good strong conker, thread a string through its centre and tie a firm knot at the bottom end. Then you were ready for battle. You could really let go of your aggression with a conker. We had a good bashing time. There was always a conker champion at the end of the day. Boys being boys we often ended up bashing each other over the head and that really hurt!

In the Autumn the Foresters used to let their pigs run free within the forest to forage for the plentiful acorns and ground nuts. The pigs gorged themselves to bursting point, their eyes bigger than their bellies. After they had been rounded up in the evening, they trotted home with a look of contentment on their faces. Poor creatures. Little did they realise that they would be presented as one of the main dishes on the Christmas table. The foresters had a code of practice when it came to the slaughter of their livestock. One owner's pig would be divided into portions and shared amongst neighbouring families and a month or two later another neighbour would do the same. It was a good repayment in kind system. Every part of the pig was used except its tail and its squeal.

The 5th of November was approaching and there was frantic activity in the forest, searching for pieces of wood for the annual garden bonfire. Each boy tried to find the best and the most wood for his own fire. There was also great rivalry among the children as to whose Guy Fawkes was the best. It depended on what materials were available. Guys were simply made and only clothes beyond repair were used. Darkness fell and the bonfire was lit. Mam and the baby were safely indoors watching the flames as they shot into the darkness. I was holding a sparkler in my hand and twirling it round and round wondering how it could possibly sparkle so. I liked the Jacky Jumpers best because they kept you guessing as to which way they would go. Unfortunately, they frightened my baby sister who began to cry and that brought events to a close.

It was seven o'clock and time for bed. The fire was still glowing in the dark as I peeped through the bedroom window.

The next morning the whole of Cinderford was enveloped by a haze of blue mist and the smell of smoke filled my lungs as I walked to school past the embers of a dozen fires.

This weekend it was decided that we lads would go chestnut hunting in the forest. The dark nights had put an end to our capers during the weekdays. The men used to take hessian sacks and collect chestnuts by the shovelful but old pillowcases were about as much as we could handle. The squirrels had already started their foraging in preparation for winter. They were cleverer than us, extracting nuts from protective prickly husks. By the end of the day our fingers were sore and painful but it was worth the suffering. We shared the chestnuts between us and headed home. Mam heated a hot plate over the fire and placed the chestnuts on the plate. The fire soon warmed them and then the shells and inner skins were easy to peel. We dipped the chestnuts in salt and they tasted delicious. The sackfuls gathered by the men were put into storage for Christmas festivities.

November mists made the forest look eerie and menacing after dark and I thought of the forest ghosts. As I lay in bed a deafening shriek rang out or a deep throated hoot could be heard close by. It made my hair stand on end as I snuggled my head under the covers. Mam told me that it was only the owls out hunting for food. I much preferred the forest in summer. The older boys used to frighten me with gory tales of horror.

"I'm not afraid," I replied. But I was.

When the curtains were drawn at night I felt safe in my castle defended by the Knights of the Round Table. No harm would come to me while Sir Lancelot guarded my bedroom door.

During the next few weeks there was frantic activity at school. Everyone was involved with preparations for celebration of Christmas, my first in the Forest. We drew, painted, cut out stars, lanterns and paper chains of different colours.

There was to be a nativity play and the teacher had to choose which children would take part. Eager hands shot up. We all wanted a part and some of us were delighted at having been chosen whilst others were disappointed. The main parts were allocated but the animal parts were still to be chosen. Some were quite happy to play the part of an animal but others were disgruntled, not wanting to be a sheep, donkey or cow.

"My sister can be baby Jesus, Miss," I said.

The teacher smiled, saying that a doll would be used. A six month old baby would be too much of a handful for the frail little girl who was chosen to be the Virgin Mary.

The last week of the school term was devoted to rehearsals for the nativity play and the Christmas carol concert. We were all given tasks as the school had to be decorated. We used the trimmings we had made. Some of the boys, under the teacher's supervision, were allowed to go into the forest to gather festive holly with brilliant berries to enhance decorations. Mistletoe was not collected. The berries were poisonous and one child would surely try to eat them. The Christmas story and the Christmas message of peace were predominant over all other lessons that week. The war in Europe over-shadowed events. Some of the boys' fathers were fighting in France so special prayers were said for them.

On the Friday morning we all assembled in the hall where a stage had been set up for the play and the scenery and props were in place. We started with the carol concert. Two of my favourite carols were, *Away in a Manger* and *Good King Wenceslaus*.

Lunchtime arrived and we all settled down to eat our sandwiches. Some were lucky as they lived near school and could go home for lunch but I always took sandwiches. The school bell rang and we stood in lines to return to the hall for the nativity play which I enjoyed enormously.

The head teacher wished us a Merry Christmas on behalf of all the teachers and said that we could go home early, which pleased us. We left school in an orderly manner as we were taught but once outside the school gates it was a different matter. We scattered in all directions heading for home.

Two weeks of freedom from the confines of the school classroom. Hooray!

6 - *Christmas Celebrations*

This year would be my sister Edytha's first Christmas. She would be six months old on 20th December. Now she was too big for her cradle. Mam used to let me nurse her occasionally but not for long as the baby was getting heavier. At times I got under Mam's feet when bad weather kept me indoors. Sometimes I would wander over to Grandfather's to see the geese, chickens and pigs but on a certain day before Christmas, when the killing started, Mam would find a task to keep me occupied so that I could not slip away to Grandfather's.

Dad went to the forest and selected a tree for our small room. There were few decorations as food was a greater priority. If there was enough money, Mam would make a fruit cake for Christmas, if not she would do the best she could. Grandmother had her own personal recipe for pudding which was a closely guarded secret. Grandfather supplied pork and chicken. There were plenty of chestnuts which had been stored since Autumn. After I went to bed, Mam would sew by the oil-lamp, making our presents for Christmas. I knew how lucky I was to get a newly altered suit or a shirt and a wooden toy.

Christmas was a simple affair for most families. Money was short but parents did their best for the children. It may have been a holiday for me and Dad but it was hard work for Mam.

Tomorrow, it will be Christmas Day. I wonder if it will snow, I thought, as I placed my sock on the bed post. I finally fell asleep and woke early on Christmas morning. I jumped out of bed and looked through the window. No, it wasn't snowing. I turned round and looked straight at my sock. It looked fatter and there was definitely something inside. This year it was an orange and some chestnuts. I liked oranges. There were no sweets because my grandmother believed that fruit was more beneficial for children.

"Pennies should be put to better use than buy sweets that rot the teeth," she would say.

My presents were under the tree downstairs with the others so I rushed down to find Mam already busy preparing chicken and pork for Christmas dinner.

"Has Father Christmas been, Mam?"

"Yes, love. Happy Christmas," she replied.

Mam picked up my presents from under the tree and gave them to me. I ripped open the wrapping paper and there was a wooden boat with a cloth sail. Great! I thought. I would be able to sail it in the brook by Grandfather's. The other present was a shirt and a pair of trousers for school.

"Thank you, Mam," I said and she gave me a big hug.

Edytha's presents were clothes too. She was growing up so fast and constantly needed larger sizes. She was too young to understand what was going on but her eyes followed Mam everywhere. Mam would perhaps have a shawl as a Christmas present, plus something she had altered for herself by hand. My father was never really interested in presents and much preferred to nip off to the local for his Christmas present. Drinks all round. Most of the men were in the local that morning. I expect the landlord did not complain.

It was very hard work for Mam but at least I was there to look after Edytha as Mam struggled to prepare the dinner. The chicken and pork were in the oven and smelled delicious. The potatoes and winter greens were bubbling away and the Christmas pudding was steaming merrily in the pot suspended over the fire. My mouth began to water in anticipation of what was to come. As soon as the pub closed for lunch, Dad would wander home for his meal. He was head of the house and it was his duty to carve the meat for dinner. Everything had to be ready upon his arrival. Dinner was served and eaten in silence. Dad would have no talking at the table. If you attempted to speak he would say, "Eat your food." A true Victorian. After dinner he would go upstairs for an afternoon nap leaving Mam and me to clear the dishes and wash up. If it was fine I used to go outside to play quietly so as not to wake Dad. Mam used to nurse Edytha in the chair by the fire and, in from the cold, I would sit at the table playing with my boat.

Dad would surface around tea time and Grandmother's pudding was ready to eat. It was delicious with sweet white sauce and went down a treat. Edytha certainly enjoyed her portion of white sauce. Dad went off to the local yet again for a drink with his pals. That's the last I would see of him until the next morning.

We were used to being together, Mam with Edytha in her arms. We would sit by the warm cosy fire singing Christmas carols. Edytha tried to join in with her gurgling sounds and occasional windy smile. Finally, she would be fast asleep and Mam would make her comfortable. We would watch the flickering flames of the fire until Mam, tired, dosed off to sleep. She did not sleep long, in case the baby woke, even though I was there to keep an eye on her. I was a big boy now and Mam used to let me stay up a little later when Dad was out. I suppose she liked the company. It must have been lonely for her when Edytha and I went to bed.

Boxing Day was a repeat performance as far as Dad was concerned and he took himself to the local. With the main cooking done yesterday, Mam decided to take us over to my grandparents' for an hour before lunch where she could have a chat with Gran. Dad was enjoying himself so why shouldn't we? Of course Grandfather was busy serving in the pub but he always found time for me. In later years I discovered that although he owned the Dog Inn he never touched a drop of beer himself. He must have been disappointed with my father and his other three sons because they all succumbed to the brew. The hour went by too quickly and we had to get back to prepare vegetables for dinner in time for Dad's return. After a silent dinner and his nap it was back to the pub in the evening. How Dad managed to go to work the next morning was a miracle, but he did!

The winter months are so depressing. I hated being stuck indoors all day looking through the window at incessant, beating rain. Some people said Cinderford was the coldest part of the Forest. Mam, Edytha and I had to brave the weather and the uphill climb to Cinderford High Street to go shopping. We got soaked to the skin struggling against wind and rain and were glad to get back to the warmth of the fire and to put our dripping wet coats over the backs of chairs to dry out.

I was keen on drawing and this was a good way to pass the time as I was bored at being confined in the house. It also great to get outside when it was fine, as long as I was dressed for the weather. My friends and I would congregate on the green and decide what we would do that day.

"Come on boys. Let's go into the forest," was the cry. Off we went, braving the cold wind blowing across open ground. Once in the forest, it felt a lot warmer. There was a deathly silence all around us. We walked along the path kicking the rotting leaves underfoot. The leaves muffled the sound of our feet and our shouts shattered the silence disturbing everything around us. A flock of blue tits flew overhead twittering in disgust. The bird which amazed me most of all was the little tree creeper. It used to start right at the bottom of the tree trunk and work its way up in spiral fashion around the trunk, picking out wintering grubs inside the bark. Unfortunately our noise frightened her away. We had a great time playing hide and seek amongst the ferns which had remained green and were ideal places to hide because they were so tall. High up in one tree we spotted a squirrel's nest, a pile of leaves and twigs nestling between the fork of two sturdy branches. Some of the boys tried to throw stones at it, although it was too high up to damage. I did not like that at all so I decided to go home.

Christmas was over for another year and soon it was 1st January, 1916. Everyone shouted Happy New Year to each other as they passed but it was not really a Happy or Peaceful New Year. The War was continuing in Europe. As a child I was not aware of this. The return to school was the main thing on my agenda. I did not mind being at school during the winter months when the weather was bad outside. The classroom fire was warm and inviting and lessons prevented boredom creeping in. I enjoyed drawing and history, especially the stories of fighting kings like Richard the Lion Heart. English and arithmetic I was not too keen on and in this I was not alone.

I longed for snow. I used to look out through the classroom window every day and pray hard for it to start snowing.

"It will come soon enough," Mam would say. "Too soon for my liking."

At last we had a heavy snowfall overnight. Dad had already left for work that morning. I so wanted to be the first to make my mark on the carpet of snow outside. Never mind, there were plenty of other stretches on which I could run on the way to school.

"Wrap up warm and be careful," Mam said.

The snow was about four inches deep, powdery and easy to walk through without slipping. It was not so easy climbing the hill to school especially when the boys were pelting you with snowballs all along the road. Sometimes their aim was accurate and a snowball would land right at the back of your neck and ice cold water would creep inside your shirt collar. It was pretty miserable then: wet all day in class. During playtime we decided to make a snowman. We were all hard at it when the bell rang. We managed to finish it the next day and were proud of our efforts. Some spoilsport knocked it all down after school. That did not deter us from starting all over again!

Snowball fights with rival gangs were great fun, although the teacher did not approve and some boys had the cane for disobedience. This was a pity as snow did not come very often and we had to make the most of it. Our joy was short-lived as the snow vanished with the arrival of cold, wet and windy weather. The dark days of winter used to make me feel sleepy, especially if there was no money to buy oil for the lamp. We had to make do with candles which gave very little light beyond the table. The light never reached the dark sinister corners of the room. Howling wind outside made the windows shake and rattle and the candles flicker, throwing ghostlike shadows around the room. I dreaded bedtime and wished I could have the candle lit all night. But that was not allowed.

February was the shortest month of the year, and the most miserable, yet the harbingers of spring, the snowdrops, began to emerge from frozen soil. The predominant colour that followed the virgin white of the snowdrops was yellow, in the abundant wild daffodils and masses of primroses that festooned the grassy banks in and around the forest. I would often pick daffodils for Mam which always brought a smile to her lovely face. Mam loved flowers.

Edytha, now nine months old, began to notice colours too and she was beginning to crawl. It was difficult for Mam to keep a constant eye on her so I kept a watchful eye, especially when Edytha would make a bee-line for the well inside the house. Edytha was beginning to talk a little, saying Mama or Dada and other unintelligible mutterings that only Mam appeared to understand. She certainly had a good pair of lungs when she let rip with crying, especially when she could see something she wanted but could not reach.

There was great excitement at Grandfather's. His brother had come to visit. Mam, Edytha and I went over to see him. There he was in the full regimental kit of the Black Watch Regiment. He had lost his leg in action and had to use crutches. Out of the whole Company, only nine men survived and all of them had suffered horrific injuries. For them, the War was over but at what cost. Yet they considered themselves the lucky ones.

It was a lovely uniform, so different from Uncle Seymour's. The jacket was black and the trousers were black and green tartan. Sometimes the soldier would wear a kilt, he said, of the same tartan. He explained that a kilt was like a skirt and the true uniform of the Scottish Clans who were fiercely proud of their dress. `The Women from Hell,' the Germans called them. It was very sad to see such a tall, smart man without his leg and reliant on crutches. Perhaps Grandmother's brother would make him an artificial leg, like his, I thought.

Everyone was looking forward to spring. The Depression had arrived in the Forest Mining Industry. Miners were used to working a five or six day week but were now working only one or two days. It was very difficult to make ends meet. As a child I was unaware of the problems my parents were facing. There was not sufficient money to pay the rent let alone to feed a wife and two growing children. There was news from Wales that things were picking up in the mines with regard to work. Dad decided once again to try his luck in South Wales, but in his heart he wanted to remain in the Forest of Dean, the place that he loved. We were to remain in Cinderford until he found work in the local coal levels and a home for the family. Leave the Forest! No! The Forest was in my heart and soul and I am still a `Child of the Forest' to this very day. It was a catastrophic blow.

"Why Mam?" I asked.

My mother sat me down and explained the necessity of the upheaval.

"We have to go love, because we need the money. The wages for two days' work is not enough to pay the rent and there is no money to buy food," Mam said.

"We can stay with Grandfather," I replied.

"No. Grandfather could not keep us indefinitely. We have to go."

I cried and cried, but to no avail.

7 - *A New School & An End to War*

My father, with his bundle of hopes and his few clothes, made his way to Ruspidge station. Goodbyes said, he was on his way to South Wales. Personal feelings had to take a back seat when it came to survival. We were to remain in Cinderford until Dad found work and a home for us. He managed to find lodgings and work in the Gelli Level at Blackwood, not far from Grandmother and Grandfather Morgan close to where we used to live before. Every week Dad sent sufficient money to pay the rent and to feed us at Cinderford whilst he continued the difficult search for a house.

One morning the letter I dreaded finally arrived.

Dad had found a house: number 38, Penybryn, Garden City (now Cefn Fforest) and he told us to prepare to move. Grindles of Cinderford carried our scanty possessions and furniture. Mam, Edytha and I were to travel down in the removal van. There were tearful farewells at Grandfather's house and I certainly cried the most as we prepared to leave the Forest that I loved dearly. Mam comforted me the best way she could by trying to cheer me up.

"It will be nice to see Grandmother and Grandfather again. I know they have missed us, Reg, and you can always come back to the Forest for a holiday," she said.

The thought that I could return to the Forest cheered me up immensely. Holidays in the Forest! Great! Maybe we would go back to live there one day, I thought. Everything was ready for the journey and the neighbours wished us all the best. Mam, Edytha and I got into the van and we were off.

There was no fear of the driver losing his way because Mam knew the route very well. Mam and Edytha sat in the front of the van with the driver. I was in the back of the van. I did not mind in the least because I had armchair comfort to watch the scenery flash by as we travelled along. The roads were narrow and twisting, especially as we approached Staunton Pitch high above the town of Monmouth where Henry V was born. The bends were so close together that with the sway of the van as it negotiated them I felt quite sick. I was glad when we reached the bottom. We then travelled towards the pretty town of Usk and headed towards Pontypool and the Welsh valleys. We passed through Crumlin,

Pontllanfraith, Blackwood and finally arrived outside 38, Penbryn, Garden City. Our new home.

It was a corner house not terraced but semi-detached with a large garden. The house was bigger than our old home and there were more windows which made it light and airy. There were three rooms downstairs, plus a bathroom with a gravity boiler for hot water which meant no more tin baths in front of the fire. There was a tap with running cold water and not a well in sight. The running water fascinated me and so did the flush toilet. No more running down the back garden in winter to go to the toilet. The master bedroom had two large windows and the two back bedrooms each had one window. There was even a small window at the top of the stairs. This was definitely an improvement on the old house. However, candles and oil-lamps were still the only form of lighting. Our furniture looked lost in the spacious rooms.

New brooms sweep clean. Mam certainly worked hard during the first week. With so many windows, curtains were essential if and when money was available. It was a good thing that Mam was clever with the needle. Financially it was a good move because Dad sometimes worked six days a week and not two days as he had in Cinderford.

In the early evening, Dad was beginning to sort out his vegetable garden so that we would have plenty of greens throughout the summer. Edytha was a bit of a handful because she had a larger area to explore now and was more adept at crawling.

By the end of the week, Mam had everything ship shape and decided to invite the family to a house warming party. Nothing elaborate, just a little gathering with tea and cakes and a tour of the house. Grandmother and Grandfather came as well as Aunty Sophia and Aunty Maud. Not interested in women's idle gossip, Dad and Grandfather slipped away to the pub.

Dad and Grandfather did not return until after Edytha's and my bedtime. The scenery was different but the old habits remained. All Mam's family lived within walking distance and she would be able to take Edytha for walks and call in for a chat. Although Mam never said anything whilst living in Cinderford, I am sure she missed her mother and sisters. There is nothing better than having your own kith and kin around you for moral support in times of trouble and need.

Once again I had to attend Fairview School. The old billy goat was still around so I gave him a wide berth. Nothing had changed except that I was a year older and beginning to understand things better. Most of my friends were still there. At least I was in familiar territory and not starting from scratch as I did in the Forest.

So it was back to the school grindstone. I could not say that I hated school but I would have preferred to be elsewhere.

"It is an essential part of your life," Mam said. "You do not want to be called a dunce and wear the dunce's cap do you?"

I persevered. Looking back, school days were certainly the best days of my life. Halcyon days with no worries or cares. We children were the innocents in a world of harsh realities. Sometimes on the way home I used to pop in to see Grandmother but did not stay too long. I had to get home before Dad otherwise he would get angry if I was not home for tea. Mam was pleased that I understood this fact because both of us would have taken the brunt of his anger.

Our immediate neighbours, Mr and Mrs Cushing, were lovely people. Rough and ready like ourselves. They had several children and had no objection to me playing with them in their own back garden. It was great having friends close at hand. Mr Cushing had fought in the Boer War in the Horse Cavalry Regiment. I was delighted when he showed me his sword and hat with a plumed feather. How exciting it all was for me. His family must have been proud of him. Across the road lived a Mrs Bevan and a Mrs Norris who were to become very good friends of Mam. We spent many pleasant hours in their company, Mam chatting and me playing in the garden. Mrs Norris had a shop and sometimes used to give me sweets from the big glass sweet jars. She was a kind and sympathetic person and came to know the problems that we had at home. Both Mrs Norris and Mrs Bevan had great respect for my mother. Poor Mrs Norris was later to lose both her legs because of a growth and finally lost her life.

A regular outing during the summer months, weather permitting, was a long walk with Grandmother, Mam and Edytha. Mam had managed to procure a secondhand perambulator as Edytha was getting too heavy to carry. We walked through Garden City, past the local woods, along narrow country lanes towards Bedwellty Church overlooking the valleys. As we approached the church my ears would pop because of the altitude. From this vantage point you could see for miles, especially on a clear day: Sirhowy, Rhymney and the Merthyr-Aberdare valleys. It was a peaceful spot and so quiet you could hear the bees buzz from flower to flower.

Grandmother was knowledgeable about wild flowers and taught me a lot. We used to pick a lovely bunch to take home as we walked along the lanes. They usually ended up looking very limp and bedraggled by the time we arrived home.

"Nothing that a drop of water won't cure," Grandmother would say.

Mam and Grandmother would enjoy their chat as we walked towards the Rock near Blackwood. For a few pleasant hours Mam could relax and enjoy the day before returning home. By this time Edytha was sound asleep.

There was always plenty of work waiting at home for Mam. How she found the strength to cope with it all I'll never know. It was real slavery. If it was not sewing, cooking, scrubbing or washing which, incidentally, was one of the worst chores of all, it was keeping a constant eye on Edytha. Poor Mam's hands were red raw from using the dolly tub and the scrubbing board. She even took in sewing and washing to help to make ends meet, especially when Dad went on one of his drinking binges and there was no money left. Yet Dad was an excellent worker. Not many men could hold a candle to him with regard to work. He was happiest amongst his old friends and cronies, drinking in the club. Behind closed doors it was a different story. Sometimes, whilst under the influence of drink, a boyish mischievousness would surface. One particular night, way past most people's bedtime, Dad decided to play the mouth organ on the green in front of the shops at 2 AM His friend Herb Davies was also there to aid and abet, singing and shouting at the top of his voice, waking everyone.

It is a wonder the neighbours did not call the police. The noise would have awakened the dead as well as the living.

Herb Davies was a real characters. His antics were an embarrassment to his wife. She was so ashamed of him that she never left the house even to do the shopping. Herb had to do all the shopping, even purchasing his wife's knickers.

One evening in the club, men started to taunt Herb, saying that he was not wearing a shirt. Herb had consumed a few drinks and was adamant that he was wearing one.

"I'll show you buggers that I have a shirt on!" he yelled. Off came his coat exposing a only white bib with a dicky bow which immediately rolled right up to his neck. You can imagine the waves of laughter throughout the club that night. He was the talk of Garden City for months. Poor Mrs Davies must have died of shame. It was nothing in those days for the average drinker to down ten to fifteen pints a night.

8 - *Hard Work and Witchery*

Mam was always working. She even had to do the decorating because if it was left to Dad it would never have been done. It was nothing elaborate, just a touch of whitewash and colouring neatly and delicately accomplished by Mam's skilful hands. During the school holidays I was glad to be able to help her by babysitting, doing odd jobs and running errands. Yet Mam never stopped me from going out to play as long as she knew where I was.

We used to play football on the green in front of the shops until some bright spark kicked the football through the shop window. We had to run or get caught. It was a long time before we showed our faces around there again. I hoped Mam would not ask me to do any shopping for a while.

Sometimes I played in the woods of the Penllwyn, near Blackwood. I used to call in on Grandmother as she lived close by and there was always a piece of cake or biscuit on offer. I liked my grandmother because she was always glad to see me and showed me great affection. On one particular visit I talked excitedly about a day trip to Barry Island that the boys had been talking about whilst playing in the woods. The trip was to be on Sunday and I was looking forward to going with them. As you can imagine, I could not wait to get home to ask Mam all about it. Yes, there was a trip, but we would not be going because there was not sufficient money to pay for the fares. My heart sank and I cried. I remained in the doldrums for the rest of the week.

"Maybe next year love," Mam said.

I was oblivious to what was going on in France. The Battle of the Somme was raging and would continue until late autumn. Life was very quiet here at home, apart from the occasional domestic squabble.

The 31st of October was Halloween, the night when goblins and witches were abroad to spread their evil. We used to call it Ducking Apple Night. Apples were placed in a bowl of water and you had to attempt to take a bite of an apple without using your hands which were placed behind your back. It was not as easy as it sounds. Sometimes you would get a mouthful of water as the apple slipped beneath the surface and you tried to grab it with your teeth. Either that or you got very wet. Trying to beat each other was great fun. It was a different matter at bedtime, when the candle was put out and I was alone in my bed. I tucked my head under the covers to hide from the goblins.

I was always glad when morning came.

There was a large house in our area called The Mansion, between the Showfield, Blackwood and Bedwellty Church. Every Christmas it was customary for the local children to be invited to call. The owner would give each child a penny or some sweets. I believe the custom dated back to the days of the old squire who lived in the area and it was still the practice when my two children were small but has now faded away. From miles around the children came, rain or shine, to collect what was on offer. No child left empty-handed. All hoped their prize would be a penny. A penny was like gold.

Edytha, now eighteen months, was old enough to appreciate Mam's carol singing. No need to say where Dad was over Christmas.

You can guess that for yourselves.

Another New Year - 1917 - not a happy one for the soldiers at War. Winter was with us again and the only thing that brightened up the dreary days of winter for me was the promise of snow and fun. Of course I used to get coughs and sniffles which made me miserable. At such times I did my best to gain Mam's sympathy and to stay home from school. Mam could always tell if I was really too ill to go to school or was playing up. God help me, though, if Dad got wind of my play acting. School was far better than a hiding.

Spring, and Dad thought it was time to initiate me into the art of gardening. He was a hard taskmaster and ruled with a rod of iron, expecting me to do every chore to his satisfaction. If I failed to pass muster he would get very angry and it would either be a hiding or banishment upstairs for the rest of the day. Sometimes both. It was agony either way. To be shut indoors and see all my friends playing outside in the sunshine was punishment enough but to get a hiding as well was unbearable. Mam did her best to shield me but she was unable to prevent it. It was not a smack with a hand but a hiding with a leather strap and buckle. I could not understand why Dad was so hard on me all the time. It was hard for Mam too. Yet she was my comforting angel. I hope that I was a comfort to her too.

Once again it was the time of year for the annual trip to Barry Island.

"Can we go this year?" I asked Mam.

"Fetch me the jar, love," said Mam.

The jar was turned upside down on the table and Mam counted the money. I waited in anticipation for her answer. When I saw her smile, I knew. Dad was not interested in the trip so it was just the three of us going. We were looking forward to our day at the seaside and the journey in a charabanc with a tarpaulin cover fitted in case of rain. And it did rain, all the way. It was still raining when we arrived at Barry Island. It was impossible to sit on the beach because it was too wet. We were huddled together in the only area under cover like sardines in a tin. The children were miserable because they could not play on the sands and the parents tried to pacify them with sweets and ice cream. Some of us decided to brave the elements to watch the Punch and Judy show. Others went to the fairground to try their luck and ride on the carousel. The women were left to look after the children whilst the men went into the nearest pub.

The sea was grey and uninviting and the waves came crashing on the shore. A few people were game enough to have a brief paddle, but not for long. Then it was a quick dash back to cover for a cup of tea and some sandwiches. By tea time most people had had enough and were ready to go home. We had to wait for the stragglers to turn up before starting back. Somebody in the group decided that we needed cheering up and started to sing popular songs. Eventually everybody joined in as we journeyed homewards. By the time we arrived home, most of the younger children were fast asleep. We looked like drowned rats. Our clothes were dripping everywhere and my white hat was flopping around my ears as the water trickled down inside my collar. Off with the wet and on with the dry was the cry when we got in the house. A quick rub down with a towel and I felt comfortable again.

This was the only outing that Mam, Edytha and I had ever been on and it had to rain.

The next important event for me was the start of my first Autumn Term in the Juniors at the big school. I was no longer an infant but a big boy now. Some of my friends came with me from the old school but all the teachers were strangers. It was the old story of starting all over again, remembering names and faces and trying to get used to them and their different ways of teaching. The best part of the move for me was the location of the school. It was only a hundred yards or so from my front door which meant that I was able to go home for lunch every day. It was at this school that I learned the art of good handwriting which appears to have fallen by the wayside. It took a lot of time and patience to achieve the skill but all my effort was worth while in the end. Even if I failed to learn anything else at school, at least I knew how to write well.

Every school had its bully and my school was no exception. There were always fights occurring in the school yard and the outcome was always the same: the cane in the headmaster's study.

I liked outdoor activities, especially football. There was a lot more to football than kicking a ball around the field. There were rules and regulations that had to be taught and explained to us by the teacher. It was a question of skill, teamwork and the love of the game, although it was nice to win too. I was always one of the first out through the doors when sports time came around. There were the usual cuts and bruises from inevitable clashes now and then but they did not bother me. I was a tough lad and could take the knocks. Mam was forever busy with the needle repairing the rips and tears that my clothes suffered as a result of my sports activities. There was no money for special football kit.

In the momentous year of 1918, the War in Europe ended. Everyone was jubilant and happy except for those who had lost loved ones. The survivors were coming home to a land `Fit for Heroes', according to the Government. Uncle Seymour and Uncle Jack came home safe and sound and had many a tale to tell the family. There were no street parties or celebrations, just a smile and a hug to show how glad you were to see them home safely. It was the War to end all Wars, the grown-ups said. They looked forward to the peace that followed. Both my uncles had difficulty readjusting to civilian life. They were soon searching for work.

There was another addition to the family in late October. My brother, Seymour, named after Mam's favourite brother. An extra mouth to feed, but very welcome. A brother to play with when he grew up, I thought. Edytha was getting under my feet now. She was nearly three and a half years old and followed me everywhere. I had great difficulty in getting away from her, especially when I wanted to go out and play with my friends. While she was occupied elsewhere I used to nip out pretty smartly and close the door which, fortunately for me, she was unable to open.

The year 1919 was uneventful. Daily life went on as usual with its trials and tribulations. I had reached the grand old age of eight and was beginning to realise that life was no fairy tale but was hard graft. Dad decided that I was old enough to take on more responsibilities and allocated me extra chores. Bucket and shovel in hand I was sent forth to comb the fields for much prized horse manure for the garden. Everyone had the same idea and it was a race to see who would be first to get there to collect the manure. Sometimes I was lucky sometimes not, which meant that I then had to go further afield. As long as I had some in the bucket to carry home I knew it would be okay. Another day would see me wandering through the local woods searching for firewood amidst the rotting trunks of the grand old man of the woods and forests, the mighty oak. I used to break up the wood, put it into the bag and carry it home on my shoulders. I made many such journeys to ensure there was enough wood to last the week.

Grandfather used to urge us not to wait until the bad weather set in but to stock up the shed with firewood during the summer months. As a child I remember that he always stated emphatically to my dad, "A roof over your head is your main concern, Sam."

"The rent first, before anything else," was another favourite phrase of Grandfather's.

At least our house was warm. Dad had a coal allowance like all miners. The allowance was despised and envied by others who did not realise the dangers miners endured to merit that allowance.

Although money was scarce, children rarely went without shoes or warm clothing. These were mostly well patched `hand me downs'. Jumble sales were a source for clothing. I was luckier than most because Mam was so clever with her needle. Looking back, I thank God for having been born into a mining community. Everybody was in the same boat. We were one great family, supporting each other through thick and thin. They were kind, decent, supportive people helping the weak to survive the hardships of life. They knew how to make the best of a harsh existence.

Their priority was that, if possible, the children should not suffer the deprivations of their grandparents and parents.

9 - *Tragedy & A Strike*

I have three vivid memories of 1920. One is painful, another embarrassing and the third extremely sad.

The first incident was at school. Like all boys I enjoyed a good climb and decided to scale the school railings which had very sharp spikes at the top like spearheads. Every class had a tale-carrier and I was betrayed to my teacher whom I was not particularly keen on. He decided to make an example of me and I was called out in front of the class. He proceeded to put me across his knee and apply the cane to my buttocks. I was only nine years old but I was pretty strong. I grabbed his legs, pulled as hard as hard as I could and watched him land on his bottom with his feet in the air. I did not wait for his or the class's reaction but bolted through the door and out of the school gates. Needless to say I did not return to school that day. I did not tell my parents for fear of my father's reaction and delayed going home until school finished for the day. On arrival at school the next morning I was ordered to the headmaster's study and duly received the punishment that I had delayed by only one day.

At the start of the new term we had a new teacher, Mrs Williams. I was very happy about this and as the weeks passed Mrs Williams and I got on like a house on fire. I thought the world of her as did the whole class. Now at last I was beginning to enjoy my lessons. A few weeks later I was summoned to the headmaster's study and entered, wondering what I had done. He asked me if I would do him a favour. I was only too pleased.

"Yes, sir," I said.

My task was to put coal on all the fires during the dinner hour. This was to be my official duty throughout the term. It was hard work for a nine year old boy.

The second incident occurred at this time. I walked into the Staff Room, bucket of coal in hand, and there was a lady teacher who had a young baby. She was squeezing milk from her breast. I could have fallen through the floor and did not know where to fix my eyes. It was the first time that I had ever witnessed this. I put the coal on the fire and with bucket in hand I closed the door and held my head down. For days and days when I passed this teacher I would lower my head in embarrassment until eventually the incident faded from my mind.

The saddest memory relates to my dear little brother Seymour who was now twenty two months old. A happy little chap, he loved music, especially the lullabies Mam used to sing. As he began to find his feet he would love to dance. One day, Edytha and Seymour were at home and Mam was busy cleaning out the ashes from the grate. She turned away for only a moment. Seymour was dancing and he tripped and fell onto the red hot coals. The screams were horrific and he suffered terribly, poor little soul. He died on the 20th August, 1920, and was buried in Bedwellty Churchyard. They say the good die young but he was only a little babe. What harm had he done to deserve such a painful death? Life is so unfair in many ways. Mam blamed herself for his death as any mother would and it must have haunted her to the day of her own death. How often I have wished that I had been at home that day to look after Seymour. God rest his little soul. He may have been alive today. Later in this sad year, Mam was to lose another child at birth, a brother, Douglas, whom we never had the chance to get to know. At least Seymour had company now, God bless them.

Christmas that year was a very subdued affair in our household. It would have been Seymour's second. One of our family was missing and we felt the loss very deeply.

"Maybe next year will be better," Mam would say.

We were all very glad when that year came to an end. People wished us a Happy New Year. We wished them the same but our hearts were not really in it. I watched Mam struggle to make ends meet. Poverty was still with us.

I managed to get an evening job with a newsagent, delivering The Argus and South Wales Echo to those who could afford them. It was only a couple of coppers but every little helped.

Edytha was now into everything and watching Mam's every move. If Mam was dusting, Edytha wanted to dust. When I did not have work to do, I had someone to play with at home.

Spring came and school nature walks began. We foraged through the woods to collect samples of plants for our studies. My home was on route and the temptation was too great. I worked my way towards the back of the group and then slipped into the house. When they returned, I would rejoin the group. Mam played hell with me.

"I'm not missing school, Mam," I would say.

I already knew about the flora and fauna from Forest days and my grandmother. Our teacher encouraged us to draw and many of my pastels of flowers and fruits of the season were displayed on the classroom walls. My own personal favourites were pansies and the basket of strawberries. This flair for art has passed down from generation to generation through my children, grandchildren and great grandchildren of whom I am very proud.

Football and rugby were my main interest at this stage. Every boy did his utmost to get selected to represent his school. The competitive spirit was intense. We all wanted to win the shield for our school. I was elated when my school won and miserable when we lost. Play for the love of the game, the teacher said, but it was every school's dream to win. We were so wrapped up in the game that we were oblivious to the rumblings of discontent between mine owners Powell Duffryn and the Miners. Men were discussing far more important issues, issues that were to affect all the mining communities in South Wales. Powell Duffryn wanted the miners to work longer hours for less pay. They had no thought for the men and their families. It was profits and costs the owners were concerned with, nothing else.

There were several meetings of the South Wales Miners' Federation in all the neighbouring valleys and the decision was unanimous. Strike action. This decision was not taken lightly. The miners had had enough. It was to be a long and bitter struggle against the owners and the miners welcomed the support of the railway workers in their fight for fair play and justice.

The month was June and the weather was beautiful. It was to be the only good thing about that year. The miners were on strike and there was no money coming in, yet the rent still had to be paid every week. There were no hand outs from the Parish and the Means Test was enforced. What decent furniture you had you were told to sell off to obtain money. Who could afford to buy the furniture? We were all in the same boat, paddling as hard as we could to keep afloat. Tough luck if you failed to sell the furniture.

To pay the rent, Mam was forced to take in lodgers. This situation was beneficial to all of us because no one could meet the full cost of the rent alone. First my Aunty Becky and her husband Dai Watkins moved in. He had served in the South Wales Borderers in the Dardanelles. He was not physically injured but was affected mentally.

"Churchill made a right bloomer of things out there," was the only remark I remember from Dai about that conflict.

Their marriage was not a happy one and living in such close proximity made it very uncomfortable for all concerned. We heaved a sigh of relief when they decided to move out. A couple with a mongol child moved in for a short time whilst they were searching for a permanent home. They were very nice people but unfortunately I cannot recall their name. When they eventually left, my Aunty Maud moved in.

Mam worked her fingers to the bone. She took in extra washing and sewing to earn a few coppers to buy what little food we could afford. There was always a sympathetic Co-operative manager who ran a much needed slate for the miners' families. He knew that all debts would be paid when the miners returned to work. Most were staunch, decent, honest hard working men. The main concern of the

South Wales Miners' Federation was the children's welfare. Soup kitchens were set up in every community. Once a day the children would arrive, bowls in hand, for a helping of soup or faggots and peas which were eaten with relish. This helped to ease the parents' worries a little. At least the children had one square meal a day.

The few leghorn chickens we possessed supplemented our meagre diet with eggs now and then. Mam would boil an egg and cut it in half, giving half an egg to me, the other half to Edytha, with a piece of home made bread. It was mostly toast and tea for breakfast. Dinner for the four of us sometimes consisted of a tin of tomatoes fried in a pan and served on a plate with a piece of bread, or stew made with a slice or two of corn beef, onions, potatoes and a bone from the local butcher with scraps of meat on it here and there. At bedtime, Mam made sure that Edytha and I had our warm cup of cocoa before we went to sleep.

Thanks to Dad's gardening expertise we never lacked fresh vegetables. Those who were unable to fend for themselves were helped by relatives and friends. Someone usually had a pig or two and when killing time arrived everyone managed to get a portion of pig.

Men who had always worked found it very difficult to adjust to the inactivity and became bored. Grown men turned to playing dominoes, cards, marbles, anything that occupied their minds. To keep up their flagging spirits, men with reasonable singing voices formed local choirs. There were contests between the choirs and the men enjoyed singing, especially the hymns which seemed to give them strength to carry on the fight.

At times of strife the Welsh have always turned to song for solace and strength.

To keep shoes on my feet, Dad used to send me to the local ash tip to look for old boots. He would remove the hobnails and use them to repair my shoes and a good piece of leather could be used as a patch.

Besides my weekly trek to gather sticks for the fire, I had to walk miles to the nearest coal tip, dragging behind me the cart that I had made myself. I would painstakingly pick lumps of coal from the tip and transport them home. It was hard, dirty work but essential to our needs.

At weekends, Mam, Edytha and I would walk five or six miles to Bargoed to do the shopping. Things were much cheaper there than in the local stores. Peglers was Mam's favourite store in Bargoed. With the little money in her possession Mam could get what we required and save a few coppers here and there. The terrain was hilly and it was hard work negotiating those steep hills and carrying the shopping home.

The personal sacrifices Mam was making for Edytha and me were beginning to take their toll and I could see that Mam was not well. Like all mothers, Mam was going without sustenance to feed us.

After one such shopping expedition to Bargoed, Dad had arrived home from the pub early and was a little tipsy. He had decided that he was going to make a stew before we arrived home with the shopping. The notion entered his head that a rabbit stew would be nice. Not realising what he was doing he killed and skinned Mam's rabbit and put it in the stew pot. By the time we arrived home, Mam was tired and exhausted. Dad proudly placed a bowl of stew on the table for her.

Mam started to eat the stew. "This is very nice, Sam," she said.

"It should be. It's your pet rabbit," Dad replied.

Mam put her hand to her mouth and ran to the toilet.

Small and frail though Mam was she lost her temper and started to throw plates at Dad. Cups and saucers went flying across the room. Dad shut himself in the pantry and Mam sat down and cried. It would be a long time before Mam began to speak to Dad. She loved that rabbit. In memory of her beautiful and much loved pet, Mam kept the pelt and mounted it on a frame. It was to be a constant reminder to Dad of what he had done.

My friends and I would sometimes decide to walk into the next valley, called the Sirhowy Valley, to swim in the river of the same name. Many local miners would congregate along the river bank and spend their time cutting their friends' hair and the children's hair, free of charge. Being a good swimmer I decided to take the plunge and dived into the river. I was swimming happily when something caught my eye. I glanced down to the river bed. Lying on the bottom was a boy who was obviously drowning and floating away with the current. I dived under and grabbed him and managed to drag him towards the bank. I shouted to some men and two of them pulled him out of the river and onto the bank. They proceeded to administer artificial respiration. Water flowed out of his mouth as they pumped his chest. Thank God he recovered. I never knew his name and was too shy to stay around to be praised for my effort. It appears that, like me, he dived in the river, but he hit his head on a stone.

It could have been me.

There was a boy called Sherby Lane who was well known in the area for sleeping rough. He even slept in an outdoor toilet one night and gave a lady a hell of a fright. He was a very difficult boy to control and his father used to thrash him with a horsewhip. Rather than go home, Sherby would kip down anywhere at night. Whenever he approached me I used to give him a wide berth because he was the type of boy who would get you into trouble. One day he tried to persuade me to go with him to the Sirhowy River.

"Don't worry, I'll get some food. Leave it to me," he said.

I refused. He was famous for going into a shop and ordering goods on someone else's bill. He knew exactly what he was doing and the shopkeepers finally cottoned on to his tricks but that did not stop him from trying it on some unsuspecting victim. The last I heard of him he had moved away to Devon, married and settled down. For the better I hope.

Sometimes I would go off with my pals to Penyfan Ponds near Oakdale. What better excuse on a beautiful hot day than to take a dip in the water to cool off. It was much better than taking a bath in hot soapy water. The water at the edge was comfortably warm but as you swam towards the centre it was very cold, so cold that it could catch you unawares and bring on cramps. I always tried to stick close to the bank. No one thought of taking food with them. One boy did bring his fishing tackle with him, thank goodness. If we managed to catch any fish we would start a fire and fry them over the open fire on sticks. If not we would gather berries, sweet leaves or even pinch the odd swede or two from the farmer's field. It was a matter of life or death for us. We were hungry. After all we had left home at nine o'clock in the morning and it was now nine o'clock at night. When I finally arrived home I wished that I hadn't. Mam gave me a ticking off. Dad gave me a hiding with his leather belt.

Not the perfect end to a perfect day.

The strike was beginning to flounder. The railway workers lacked the courage to continue the strike and returned to work. Once the railways were transporting stocks of coal, the miners' strike was doomed. They held out for as long as they could, but extreme poverty and suffering forced them back to work under those terrible conditions. Powell Duffryn had no thought for the men, slogging their guts out, or for their families. Powell Duffryn had no soul and it was cheap labour for them. The owners walked out on Sunday with their well-dressed, well-fed families whilst I walked about in patched up clothes and patched up shoes.

Snobs we called them. Rabble they called us.

The government brought out the troops to subdue us. Wales has always been socialist and the Welsh firm supporters of the Labour Party. It was the only Party that understood the sufferings and hardships of Welsh Valley folk. We hated and despised Powell Duffryn and the Tories. God how they must have laughed at us. Memories of their outrages are still as vivid today as they were then. Socialist I am and socialist I remain. They will never change my mind, body or soul.

10 - *One Flame Flickers, Another Dies*

After twenty long weeks the strike ended and the miners returned to work, defeated but not humiliated. They fought for a principle and lost but the fight was not going to end there. They were forced to accept longer hours for less pay but did it for the sake of their families. Old wounds ran deep and they were not going to take things lying down. They would try again when the time was ripe. Hatred of the employers was embedded as deep as the coal. It would be many months before debts incurred during the strike were paid. The people to whom the miners owed money were more sympathetic to the miners than the employers.

Dad returned to the Gelli Level at the coalface and although the wage was less, there was more money available for Mam to pay the bills and feed us. Mam did not look well and was very pale and wan. I knew something was wrong and I did my best to help her. Mam was of small build and not strong yet she and I would still walk those five or six miles to Bargoed in wind, rain, sleet and snow to save a few coppers to pay off debts. The money in the jar on the mantlepiece was not savings for Christmas or the annual outing but for the debts. The struggle during the miners' strike had taken its toll. I watched Mam as she laboured to make ends meet. It was far from easy for the women folk to clothe and feed their families on that money. Mam's life was not a bed of roses. Her friends and family knew this and all had great respect for her.

Mam was a lady.

On one particular weekend I happened to glance at Dad's pay docket which was lying on the table. I may have been only ten and three quarter years old but I realised that the money Dad gave Mam did not add up to the figure on that docket. I mentioned it to Mam but it did not alter the situation one little bit. In those days husbands gave their wives what they thought was sufficient for housekeeping. The women had no say in the matter.

"When I am old enough to work, Mam will get all my wages," I thought to myself.

It would help her to cope with the bills and buy little extras for all of us. Having seen how she struggled and suffered it was very hard to forgive Dad for holding back that money. It was unfair of him because that extra money would have helped to ease Mam's constant worries.

Life went on as normal with our daily struggle for survival. Mam seemed to be getting more tired as the weeks passed. I soon realised why. She was expecting another child in April.

On 15th April, 1922, the day before my eleventh birthday, my baby brother Merlin was born. What a wonderful near birthday present Merlin was for me. At the time my thoughts, and Mam's and Dad's too I'm sure, were of my little brother Seymour. His memory was still fresh in all our minds. As Merlin grew up we were all over-protective of the little chap. He seemed a healthy baby but suffered a double rupture, which was to plague him for quite some time. He had to wear a support, but in spite of his incapacity he remained a pleasant little chap.

At the end of the school term it was decided that I was to spend some time at my grandfather's in the Forest of Dean. Dad took me to Cinderford by train and then returned home. How would Mam manage without me, I thought. Edytha was now seven and old enough to help, so that eased my mind a little. I met up with old pals and revisited my haunts in the Forest. It was great to be back but I missed my mother.

My stay was to last about three months or so and there was no getting out of school either, worse luck. During the school holidays, Grandfather gave me chores. The main one was to polish his leather leggings for his work on the railway. Boy did I make them shine. I also fed his many animals and learnt the art of gardening. He took pride in his garden as all market gardeners do and it was a joy to see. There were very few chemicals in use in those days. Natural predators and soapy water did the job.

There was one particular brush with a now very famous celebrity. His name was Jimmy Young. Yes, the famous Jimmy Young of *Unchained Melody* fame, not a bad singer either. His parents' home was close to where my Aunty Edith Ruck lived in Cinderford. It was Sunday evening and as I was leaving my Aunty's home, Jimmy, who was playing on the Green in front of his home, approached me. His parents had gone to the local Methodist Chapel in Church Road, Cinderford which had been paid for and built by the miners. Mrs Young was a music teacher and played the organ at chapel. Mr Young worked in Lightmoor Colliery in the Forest a few miles away.

"Come on, Reg, let's pinch some of my mother's apples. It will be alright. Mam and Dad are in chapel," said Jimmy.

I was taken aback to think that he was like that at all. But if Jimmy said it was alright and they were his own apples, then why not? We picked some apples then went on the Green to eat them. The apples were delicious, sweet and juicy. Jimmy was always the dandy boy and I can see him now, dressed in his knickerbocker suit with his little school cap on his head. The boys used to snigger yet he was always regarded as one of the lads, mischievous as the rest of us. His clothes may have been different, but he was one of us.

In October it was decided that I was to go home before the dark nights of winter set in. Much as I loved the Forest, I was homesick and missed Mam and my family. Grandmother and Grandfather were good to me but it was not the same. I made myself a promise that I would return to the Forest one day.

Dad and I settled down for the journey to South Wales. The autumn colours were at their very best as we chugged along. My thoughts were in unison with the rhythm of the train.

"I'm going home, diddle de de. I'm going home, diddle de da, diddle de de, diddle de da."

The mountains of South Wales were on the distant horizon and I knew that I was nearly home. I sat back, content in the knowledge that I would soon see Mam and the children. It was a long walk from the station and I thought we would never get there. The longest mile is the last mile home, as the saying goes. It was early evening by the time we arrived and I could see that Mam was pleased to see me. We gave each other a great big hug. Edytha was delighted, too. Merlin was now a bonny six month old baby. How he had grown in those few months. He was certainly a happy child.

It was great to be home.

Everything had been prepared for winter. The shed was stacked with firewood which was a relief as I did not fancy combing the woods in winter.

Money was tight but Mam had managed to repay most of the debts which had accumulated during the strike. She must have worked unceasingly to achieve this. Edytha was proving useful to Mam around the house but the only time Mam had any relaxation was late evening when the baby was settled down, but never out of sight. Edytha and I used to play with the candle making warts on our hands until we were reprimanded by Mam. Sometimes we played with our collection of cigarette cards - the poor person's equivalent of stamp collecting.

Even though Dad delegated more work to me now I still managed to go to the woods with my friends occasionally. On one such exploration my curiosity got the better of me. As I wandered through the woods I spotted a tree with a large hole in the trunk. I put my arm, right up to the armpit, into the hole. Something inside bit deep into my fingers. My arm came out quicker than it went in. My fingers, bleeding, were gripped by a bat, its teeth well dug in. Removing the culprit was a slow and painful process. Once bitten, twice shy. It was the first and last time I put my hand in any dark and mysterious place.

I was now twelve years old and beginning to dislike girls intensely. Edytha wanted to come with me when I went off with the boys across the fields and hills. Girls play such sissy games. I wanted to fly through the trees like a monkey or play tricks on people. There was one particular stunt that the boys and I used to pull. We would place a stick reasonably firmly against a window and tie a long piece of cotton to it, then hide in the bushes close by. With the other end of the cotton in our hand, we pulled gently and the stick would tap the window-pane. The occupier would come out with a puzzled look on his or her face, see nothing and probably assume that it must have been the wind. We tried it once too often and they got wise to us. If Edytha, or any other girls, had been with us our parents would have been sure to find out, resulting in a hiding and banishment to the bedroom. In her innocence, Edytha always told the truth and that's how I used to get into trouble. A boy has to do what a boy has to do. A brother is best, a sister's a pest. Where had I heard that before, I wondered.

It is funny how you can go off girls.

The following year was to bring another addition to our ever increasing family. My sister Beryl was born late 1924. Now we were four. With an extra mouth to feed, things were getting tougher for Mam who was trying to cope to the best of her ability. Merlin was two and a half years old and with Beryl a babe in arms it was putting a terrible strain on Mam's stamina. The shopping expeditions became an even greater struggle and I could see that Mam's health was failing.

School life was almost over for me. Soon I would be fourteen and earning a wage. It was every boy's dream to finish school and start work. More so for me because I knew it would be of great benefit to Mam.

Little did I realise how tough a miner's life would be. I can honestly say that for all the years I worked in the mines I hated every moment.

Circumstances dictated my occupation There were no other opportunities in the valleys at that time. It is even worse today because all the mines have gone and there are no other industries to take their place.

As my fourteenth birthday approached, Mam's health deteriorated. I was very worried about her. Dad had arranged for Aunt Sophia to look after her whilst he was working and insisted on paying my aunt a fee for her services. He was very independent that way. The day after I finished school I started work with my father in Gelli Level. It was very cold and damp in that level. Dad expected a man's work from a fourteen year old boy. My first task was to fill a tram with coal. I did not fill it quickly enough to satisfy Dad and he became impatient with me.

"Never let your mother know that she bred a jibber," he said. This phrase was indelibly printed in my mind and still is to this very day. I have never been a shirker and the accusation was unjust. Throughout my life I have never `jibbed' but always gave my employer more than a good day's work. Dad was a hard man to satisfy, but to his credit he was a good worker.

The day I started work, the child within me died.

Mam's condition grew steadily worse and the doctor was called to the house. The diagnosis was rheumatic fever. Mam was in excruciating pain and could not bear anyone to move or touch her. What had she done to deserve such agony?

Mam's screams pierced my heart and I cried. Mam's hair had always been her crowning glory and it had to be cut short because she could not be moved to wash it. When my aunt was not there I used to sit by Mam's side and sometimes she would ask me to fetch some water from the spring across the field.

Anything for you Mam. Anything.

The water was cool and comforting. As I lifted the glass to Mam's mouth, she would smile and say, "Thank you love," even though the effort caused her pain.

Sometimes Dad would sit with her, and Edytha and I were again sitting at the table playing with a candle. As the candle flickered I heard a noise which made me look towards the door. In the doorway was an outline of a woman which looked like my mother. I knew deep down inside that it was a bad omen. I did not say anything to my sister because she would have been afraid. The next morning Mam passed away. Her dying thoughts were of me, so I was told.

"What's going to happen to Reg now?"

Mam was thirty four years old and left a six month old baby, Beryl, a three year old, Merlin, and Edytha, aged ten. I was fourteen.

My world collapsed. The light of my life was extinguished forever, like a candle flame by the wind. Oh Mam! Why? Why did you have to die and leave me? Please God, say it's not true. You did not deserve to die so young.

Being the eldest, my memories are very clear of Mam who was always a caring, devoted mother. She unselfishly thought of her children before herself. She deserved a much longer, happier life. Most of her brothers and sisters lived well into their nineties. In fact, her sister Maud is still alive. I blamed Dad for Mam's death. I felt that if Mam had been treated properly her life would have been different. At the time I did not realise Mam's death had brought Dad to his senses. He realised his loss too late and blamed himself. He never remarried and Mam's death was to haunt him all his life. As I grew older I grew wiser and realised that you could not bear a grudge forever, although it was many years before I finally forgave him. On my last visit before Dad passed away aged eighty nine, my wife Phyllis and daughter Elaine accompanied me to Cinderford. They sat at his bedside. I was chatting to my brother Merlin.

"I think I've suffered enough for what I have done," Dad said to Phyllis.

Phyllis replied, "Yes Dad, you have."

I am glad that I made my peace with Dad during his final years.

My mother was laid to rest with her children, Seymour and Douglas, in Bedwellty Church - united in death, God rest their souls.

My Uncle Jack made a beautiful cross in oak and placed it on the grave for us. I attended the funeral, comforted by all the family and friends including our relatives from the Forest of Dean. I had to say my last goodbye to Mam. Dad was in a dilemma. What was he to do with very young children bereft of their mother?

Aunty Edith, Dad's sister from Cinderford said to Dad, "Look, Sam, if you are willing I will take baby Beryl home and bring her up as my own."

Dad thought about it and agreed this was the best course of action. Beryl went out of our lives and settled down with her adopted family. My Aunty Edith had a heart of gold. She already had four children of her own. Three weeks after Mam was laid to rest, Dad decided to pack up and return to Cinderford.

"I don't want to die here in Wales. I'm going back to the Forest," he said.

11 - *Return to the Forest*

I had wanted to return to the Forest of Dean, but not under such sad circumstances as this. Grandfather provided a home for us in one of the houses that he owned. It was not home to me but an empty shell.

The foundation stone was missing - Mam.

The heart of a family is the mother. Once that heart has stopped things are never the same. Grandfather in Wales had said, "A roof over your head is your main concern, Sam." That's all our new house represented for me. There was no welcoming smile to greet me, just a cold, empty hearth. Mam wasn't there to listen to my troubles and give me comfort. Many a night I cried myself to sleep, but I did not cry in front of Dad. Sometimes during the day I would go off into the forest and find a quiet spot where I could weep alone. I did not want anyone to see me crying.

There would be many a time when I would seek the solace of the forest to hide my grief.

For six weeks Dad made no attempt to search for work. He was probably trying to come to terms with Mam's death. Grandfather realised this and persuaded Dad to take an interest in pig breeding. Being a market gardener and pig breeder, Granddad had two sizeable fields to accommodate the pigs.

"Try them, Sam," he said.

Soon we were the proud owners of eight Gloucester pigs. Most were white, apart from one or two who were white with big black spots. It surprised me that they were clean and slender, not my usual picture of a pig. I always thought they were dirty creatures but I was wrong. I was no longer afraid to feed them, although I must confess they were not yet fully grown. I became extremely fond of them and learnt a surprising amount about pigs in the first six weeks. Vegetable waste was collected for their feed - cabbages, small potatoes, swedes, beans and barley meal sharps (a mixture of barley and fine oats) were boiled in twelve four foot high tubs giving us lots of pigswill. An aunt who owned a fish and chip shop kept scraps for us, which the pigs loved. I would watch them scratching around the field with their snouts, squealing in excitement when a source of food was discovered. They delighted in having their backs scratched.

This was sheer bliss for them. The thought of killing was far from my mind as they were like pets to me.

Grandfather's sow was expecting and we all waited with great anticipation. How many piglets would she have? Would we need to bottle feed the runts of the litter? Each morning I would rush out for the latest report from Grandfather, only to return disappointed. The days dragged on and still there was no sign of piglets. As farrowing time approached the sow was getting hot, restless and irritable. One day she had had enough and decided to vent her anger on me. She almost flew at me and hit the pen door, shaking it violently. I thought it would break under her brute force but it withstood the assault. She usually had such kind and friendly eyes but now they blazed with hatred.

"We must keep our distance," I told my sister, who was small and thin.

Edytha scattered corn for the chickens, collected eggs from the hen-house, and, on my advice, gave the sow a wide berth.

In the meantime, what little money Dad had was running out. He decided it was time to find employment at Lightmoor Colliery which was within easy walking distance of Cinderford. I found work there too. Arrangements were made for Edytha, who was back at school, and Merlin, who was three years old, to be cared for by my grandmother during the day. Grandfather had retired from the railways and would look after our pigs, his own, and the expectant sow. At least there were no worries at home whilst Dad and I went to work. Little did I realise how close to slavery work in the Forest mines was to be. I would soon find out.

Dad and I would be working as a team. I was Dad's helpmate, called the hodder, the first job allocated to an inexperienced newcomer. Namely me. The seams of coal were only eighteen inches high and you had to crawl on hands and toes dragging the coal behind you. The roof was so low that you could not kneel without your back becoming wedged against the roof. The hodder was the human equivalent of the horse. My job was to pull a coal laden hod, something like a snow sleigh, along rough ground thirty or forty yards. I wore a harness with straps over my shoulders and a chain hooked up between my legs. Eight hours a day I struggled to and fro dragging the coal behind me. The leather straps dug into my flesh and the friction made my shoulders red-raw. It was agony. I listened to some advice from the old-timers who said that rubbing your own urine into your shoulders would help harden your skin and toughen it up. Salt water and methylated spirits were good too.

From the very first day in the mine I hated every second spent there and every yard I winced with pain. But I did not betray my suffering to Dad.

At the coalface the only means of light for the miners was the naked flame of a candle wedged into a lump of yellow clay and pressed into the timber post supporting the roof. The actual coal face was very often a mile or two from pit bottom. It was too low for man or beast.

Horses were employed underground in this colliery and in Crump Meadow Colliery, but in many of the Forest mines the roadways were inaccessible to our four footed creatures. In the main roadways the smaller pit pony was employed to pull the trams to the parting which housed the full trams and the empty trams. The full trams in the parting were then hitched up to the steel rope on the haulage wheel at one end, called the tail rope, and the haulage drum at the other end, called the main rope, for transportation by the haulage driver to pit bottom. The haulage was controlled by means of a brake operated by the haulage driver to prevent overshooting. The empty trams were then hooked up and taken to the workings by the same means. Sometimes the steel rope fell short, preventing the hitch up of the trams. It was then that the strength of the magnificent shire horses was employed to pull the rope to link up the trams. Needless to say this type of haulage was called the Main and Tail Haulage.

Once a week, at the end of the shift, explosives were used to give the hodder sufficient height to continue his work during the next few days. It was dangerous work and left in the capable hands of more experienced miners like my father. By using a stand machine, fixed in position between the floor and roof, holes could be bored. To position the hole correctly, the machine had an adjustable clamp which slid up and down. Attached to this was a traveller or screw thread enabling a drill to be placed at one end and a handle to be fixed to the other. If the rock proved too hard, a ratchet had to be applied and if space was limited the handle could not be turned. If this was the case, a second ratchet would be attached and by a pushing and pulling motion the hole could be drilled. It was essential to keep sufficient height for the horses, whose heads would rise upwards to the roof under the strain of pulling the loaded trams. A short drill was applied in the initial stage and when it had reached its own length in the hole, a second drill was used until the correct depth was reached. A copper rammer was used to place the charge into the hole and a copper needle was then placed down the hole. This needle was between three and three feet six in length, depending on the depth of the charge required. The hole was then very carefully packed with clay and once sufficient clay had been rammed down the hole the needle was withdrawn leaving a hollow channel leading down to the charge. A squib shaped like a rocket firework was the detonator and when lit and placed in the hole, travelled down by its own propulsion and ignited the gunpowder.

The nightmare for me and the other unfortunate hodders was that our task the next day was to clear all the rubble brought down by the charge. For every hod of rubble cleared a hod of coal had to be brought from the coalface. I was glad when the shifts and the first week ended. I did not look forward to next week's work, or any other week's. Slavery had to be better than this, I thought.

There was no choice. It was work or starve.

THE HOD

THE LEATHER HOD STRAP THAT FITTED OVER THE MINER'S SHOULDERS

In Dad's opinion I was now a grown man. Yet the thought of next week's work brought tears to my eyes, which I did not let him see.

The week's work had ended. I walked wearily home. I was elated by the thought that for two whole days mine and work could be forgotten. I was able to stand erect and breathe in God's fresh air. I had plenty of work to do at home but this was heaven compared to hodding.

Dad was a pretty good cook but he gradually handed over that responsibility to me. It was plain, simple fare, nothing fancy. I tried hard to remember the meals Mam used to make for us and the method she used in preparing them. During the day I tended the vegetable patch, trying hard to keep the dreaded weeds under control. Edytha was a proper little housewife and a mother to Merlin which seemed unfair because she was only ten years old. In the evening before Dad went to the local for his usual draught we had to feed and water the pigs who were growing at a rapid pace. Edytha tended the chickens and collected eggs. Chores completed, we spent an hour or two with Grandmother before returning home.

Sunday mornings were mainly devoted to the preparation of dinner. Edytha and I would clean the vegetables whilst Dad attended to the meat. His favourite was pork. It was surprising how many meals we could have from one pig. After the pig had been killed, Grandmother would remove the chitterlings wash and clean them, turning them inside out with a long stick to ensure they were clean. She would then boil them and leave them to cool for supper. We had belly pork, boiled pigs' trotters, and brawn made from the pig's head, which I thoroughly enjoyed.

At home Dad had a wooden bench where he prepared sides of bacon, home-cured by saltpetre. Then he would wrap it in brown paper and hang it on hooks in the cellar. When it was ready, all we had to do was cut off a slice with a sharp knife. The bacon was so firm it stood on end, not like the floppy bacon you get in the shops today. There is one butcher's shop in Cinderford, Masons, which still practises the old method of home-curing bacon.

After dinner, if it was fine, Edytha, Merlin and I would go for a walk through the forest. We took turns to carry Merlin if he got tired of walking. He was often asleep before we arrived home for tea. Once, at Grandmother's whilst collecting eggs, we heard a loud commotion from the pig-pen. We peered gingerly over the wall at the sow. She was pushing the feeding trough around the pen and trying hard to lift it off the ground. She was angry and when she saw us she came straight for us. We jumped back and as we ran passed her gate it groaned and creaked as she threw herself at it. We thought she would break out and ran to Grandmother's where we remained until Dad and Grandfather returned from their walk. We blurted out what had happened then left the sow in the capable hands of the experts. There were squeals, grunts and shouting for about an hour. Then Dad returned.

"Her ordeal is over," he said. "She has had her litter."

We were not too keen to approach the pig-pen that night!

Sunday evening soon became night and I did not relish the thought of work next morning. It was Monday blues all week but there was no time to reflect or feel sorry for myself. It was hard slog day in day out. After my evening chores at home I was too tired for anything else. I lived for the weekends because sometimes, if Dad agreed, I managed to get away with my friends.

It was high summer and the fruit season. Popes Hill, famous for Victoria plums, was the place to be. We decided to go fruit hunting and took some old pillowcases along with us to carry the fruit.

The first to get there got the best pickings. One lad got there ahead of us. As we approached he started jumping around as if he had St Vitus Dance or ants in his pants.

"What's wrong with him?" I shouted.

We soon found out. It wasn't ants in his pants but wasps swarming all around him. He had disturbed their nest. The wasps not only took their revenge on him but on us as well. We did not get any plums that day. We just ran hell for leather out of there, to the delight of the owners.

Never mind, there was always another day.

"Serve you right," Dad said.

It was August and mushroom time. I adored mushrooms and would go out into the forest searching as if prospecting for gold. You had to know what you were about as many toadstools looked similar to mushrooms. To be poisoned was the last thing I wanted. I was too young to die.

On my travels I would often come across gypsies, or didicoys as we used to call them, camping in the Forest, real Romany gypsies with their traditional caravans so beautifully carved and decorated. They were very friendly. When I was in the area they would invite me to have a meal A large black cauldron hung over the wood fire. Every kind of vegetable was tossed into the pot as well as rabbit or hedgehog meat. It looked a mess but was delicious. The gypsies always got the blame when chickens went missing but this was sometimes an unfair accusation. More frequently the locals were the culprits.

The gypsies' presence in the village made Saturday exciting. The locals and the gypsies used to frequent the same pubs. Trouble would flare up over some remark. A fight would start and blood would flow. The gypsies carried their knives as a cowboy would carry his six-shooter. We lads thought it was great fun and entertainment as we sat on the wall observing. It added a bit of spice to the normally dull and unexciting life of the village. The gossip lasted for days and days. Of course after this kind of trouble the gypsies were moved on whether or not it was their fault. I was sad to see them go.

"See you next year!" they shouted.

Autumn was soon upon us and the threat of winter was in the air. It was time to gather in wood to last through winter. We went to work in the dark and came home in the dark.

There were no daylight hours in the mine, just the light from the candles we carried with us.

The elements unleashed their fury. Rain and wind lashed us on the way to work You were soaked to the skin before you arrived at the mine and the frost pierced your very soul. The day's hard graft kept me warm and there was no time to worry about the weather above ground. I was always glad to get home and shut out the cold, even though the fire had to be lit and encouraged to burn. Hot water was the next priority, to wash off the sweat and grime from the day's work. Dad and I took turns in the tin bath in front of the fire. Dinner was next, usually a stew prepared the night before and ready to heat up over the now roaring fire. Edytha would arrive home from Grandmother's with Merlin, or sometimes Mrs Bishop would bring Merlin across. Between Grandmother and Mrs Bishop, Merlin was well cared for and we knew that he was in safe hands. Mrs Bishop was a wonderful person and a great help to the family. How kind people were in those days.

After dinner, Edytha and I would settle down to a game of Snap, or try to keep Merlin amused until bedtime. On rare occasions I managed to get away to the cinema if funds allowed.

Dad still loved to frequent local pubs. He could be difficult in drink, impishly mischievous Once at 2 AM I was awakened from my sleep.

"You watch this, Reg. I'll get him next door going," Dad said - the worse for drink.

He took his mouth organ and started to play close to the partition wall. Every tune in his repertoire, including the Welsh hymns. Hidcock, the man next door, got up and started to sing at the top of his voice, much to the annoyance of the neighbours. Dad was oblivious to all that and was enjoying every moment. Another time his drinking pals would stay late, testing Dad's home-made wines, which were very potent. They were inevitably in high spirits and caused the neighbours a sleepless night. The long-suffering neighbours finally found it all too much and complained to Grandfather who was the landlord. He was a very proud man and when the complaint was laid before him he confronted Dad.

"You'll have to go Sam, if thou doesn't stop your nonsense and mend your ways," he said.

"It's only a bit of fun, Dad," was the reply.

"That's not the point, Sam. Folks round here need a decent night's sleep," said Grandfather.

Dad mended his ways. For a while.

Sometimes, after Dad had gone to the pub, my pals would drop in. This gave me the opportunity to show off my talent for playing the mouth organ. If Merlin was asleep, the four of us would take a candle in a jam jar and go into the communal toilet which was across the lane from the house. Edytha was left to look after Merlin. What a place to choose. There was no flush and bowls of water had to be used to clear it all away. Unfortunately for me we did this once too often. The toilet had a long wooden seat with the necessary hole in the centre. While my pals sat on the floor, I stood on the seat playing the mouth organ and dancing left of centre stage on the top. One night the seat broke. Down I went straight into the cesspit, shit and all. My pals deserted me as I struggled to get out. Expecting a hiding off Dad I groped my way to the brook across the road to wash myself and my clothes. I felt like an outcast for a while and realised why the skunk was shunned.

Never again. The broken toilet seat remained an unsolved mystery to the toilet users. Only my pals and I knew the secret and we were not going to tell.

Our first Christmas without Mam just wasn't the same. I was glad when it was all over and done with. For Merlin's sake, Dad, Edytha and I put on a brave face but our thoughts and feelings were in Bedwellty Churchyard at the grave-side of the person dearest to our hearts. Mam and the two little ones with her.

"Maybe things will be better next year," echoed through my mind.

"No, Mam, not this time," I thought.

I cried myself to sleep that night. I never thought I would be glad to return to work, but the sooner the better. At least there my mind was fully occupied.

"Happy New Year!" everyone shouted.

Little did they realise the trouble that was brewing in the mining communities of South Wales and the Forest of Dean.

The year was 1926.

12 - *1926*

The year started well enough. Both Dad and I had regular employment and wages coming in. I never found out how much Dad's wages were but mine were three shillings and sixpence a week. (Seventeen and a half pence). With all our hardships we made our own happiness, simple though it was, and this included enjoying our time outdoors.

Sometimes when it was cold and frosty but fine, we would take a walk in the forest. How different it was in winter months. Its character had changed completely. The deciduous trees bereft of leaves looked stark against the sky line. It was a cold and uninviting place except for the mighty firs resplendent in their coats of dark forest green. They provided plenty of cover for birds. The robin broke the deathly silence with its beautiful song. How creatures managed to defeat the harshness of winter was a miracle to me. Yet survive they did. The bracken provided shelter for the hibernating creatures. I envied them their long winter sleep.

To miss winter and wake up in spring - sheer bliss!

Our forays into the forest held many a surprise as we wandered along its rambling pathways. The bright berries of a holly tree lifted our spirits and dispelled the winter blues. Red is such a vibrant and warm colour - just what you need on a winter's day. It was even more captivating when virgin snow fell and carpeted the entire forest.

Animal tracks abounded, imprinting the soft powdery snow. The Sherlock Holmes in me surfaced as I tried to guess which creatures the paw and hoof prints belonged to. I even followed tracks in the hope of finding an answer. But the creature was either long gone or safely hidden.

The grey days of winter soon gave way to the fresh greens and yellows of spring, promising better things to come. Or so we thought.

My fifteenth birthday was fast approaching and for the very first time in my life I fell deeply in love. With the Motorbike. My cousin Sammy had a Douglas belt drive bike with a flat petrol tank. We became partners in this beautiful machine and at weekends used to travel from Cinderford to Gloucester or to Monmouth via Staunton Pitch, notorious for its many bends. It was not easy to negotiate these bends on a motorbike and I clung for dear life to Sammy with my heart in my mouth and butterflies in my tummy. Boy was I glad to reach Monmouth. I certainly wasn't looking forward to the return journey. There were plenty of open roads in the Forest and very little traffic. I guess we were real tearaways as we let rip along the roads, foot-loose and fancy free. Wandering sheep were the greatest danger. The partnership did not last long because I could not maintain my share of expenses. Sammy eventually took over complete ownership of the bike. Like me, he had started work in the mines but then took a job at an aeroplane company in Gloucester, hence his need for the bike.

My love for the motorbike never died and I still have fond memories of that wonderful machine.

Come April, Sammy decided that it would be a good idea for me to witness the famous River Severn Bore. It was an experience I will never forget. The river is tidal and at the highest tide of spring a sight to watch with awe. A thunderous roar could be heard some distance away towards Newnham, becoming louder as it thundered along the river's course until it finally came into view. A great tidal wave of white horses came sweeping up the river, lashing the sides of the river's banks and engulfing them completely by raising the water level eight feet or more. Crowds lined the bank, keeping a safe distance. If you were too near the bank you could be swept away by the force of the tidal wave. It even flooded low lying meadows and farmers had to make sure their stock was safely out of harm's way. Ferry men were out of pocket for a short while but once the danger was past they did exceedingly well plying people across the River Severn, cutting short a journey of many miles from Newnham across to Berkeley Castle.

Below Newnham, the Severn Railway Bridge spanned the river from Blakeney to Sharpness Docks enabling coal from the Forest mines to be transported to the docks for export. The River Severn in its heyday was a very busy and active thoroughfare even in my youth. It was also a favourite spot for swimming, but it was no place for the weak swimmer or the faint hearted. The Severn was a fast flowing river. Swimmers had to be careful where they entered because the current could sweep you hundreds of yards down river in no time. Above Newnham towards Westbury-on-Severn the river was famous for its elvers, baby eels. These were a real delicacy to the connoisseur and just as delicious to us. A special net was used to catch them as they congregated near the river bank. We would put them in a container and carry them home where they were boiled or fried. In the process of cooking they turned milky white and were devoured with great relish. Grandfather told me how in his youth the river froze during a very bad winter and the ice was so thick an ox could have been cooked on its surface. This tall story turned out to be true.

We two April boys celebrated our birthdays. Merlin was four years old on the 15th and I was fifteen on the 16th. It was almost a year since Mam's death.

Merlin was a grand little chap. Mam would have been proud. Around this time there were rumblings of discontent in the mining industry in Wales. Yet another confrontation was looming between miners and coal owners. Coal exportation was in decline and mine owners throughout the country expected miners to work longer hours for less pay. Naturally this was unacceptable to the miners and they refused outright.

"Not a minute on the day, not a penny off the pay," was the cry.

On 1st May, 1926, the mine owners decided to take drastic action and prevent the miners from working by means of a lockout. The Welsh first, followed by the rest of the coalfields. After this lockout, the Trade Union Congress decided to call a General Strike from 3rd May. Key industries such as the railways, docks, gas and electricity were called out. Not all industries joined the miners' stand. As in 1921, the protest was short lived and the General Strike ended on 13th May, 1926.

"Betrayal!" was the cry.

The miners felt the trade unions had let them down yet again. Throughout the land the mining communities were angry but we were determined to go it alone as we had done before. The Miners' Federation was unable to support its members financially as funds were not available and once again the Parish would only provide for wives and children. Kind decent folk sympathetic to the miners' cause rallied round with voluntary contributions. Soup kitchens sprang up. The months dragged on - June, July, August. A contingent of miners from Cinderford and surrounding areas decided to go on a hunger march to the Westbury-on-Severn Workhouse four or five miles away. Dad decided that we would join them and on the day we marched as one, united in our aim. On arrival we each received half a loaf of bread, a piece of cheese and a cup of cocoa. We felt like beggars and Dad's pride was hurt.

"Never again, Reg," he said. "I'm a free miner with rights and I know where to find a seam of coal."

The degradation of begging at the workhouse was too much to bear.

The seam of coal that Dad discovered was close to Dilkes Hospital which was started from funds raised by the miners firstly from Lightmoor Colliery and then from the surrounding collieries. A hospital is essential in a mining area because of the serious accidents which sometimes occur in the industry. The seam of coal was only ten feet down from the surface and therefore reasonably accessible. The first thing on the agenda was to find a coal merchant. This meant Dad had to travel to Gloucester to make the necessary arrangements. The merchant would provide the trams transported by rail from Gloucester to Ruspidge Station and we would supply the coal to fill those trams. The financial details were agreed between the merchant and Dad and we were in business. At last we had some money coming in to keep us going until the strike was settled.

When that would be we did not know. Dad and I continued to work this seam successfully throughout the autumn.

It was hard graft and Dad was a tough taskmaster but anything was better than begging for food at the workhouse.

The miners' stand began to waver in December, 1926 and the Federation, against all principles, finally accepted defeat. The Speech House was the venue for a meeting between the union and the mine owners.

"There can be no compromise. Accept our terms as they stand," the owners demanded.

They were adamant and would not bend. The miners reluctantly accepted their terms. There was nothing to be achieved from further conflict. Eight hard gruelling months. For what? It was the principle of the thing that miners fought for. A decent wage for an honest day's work. We weren't asking for the moon.

Dad and I went back to Lightmoor Colliery but many miners did not return to the Forest mines. The year was nearly over but not forgotten. Miners were bitter and their memories long. The lessons learned from this conflict were embedded deeply in their minds for future confrontations which would surely come.

They say that history often repeats itself. Not too often, I hope.

Within a few weeks Dad left Lightmoor Colliery to work in the New Fancy Colliery close to the Speech House. The pay was better for his line of work but not for mine. I was left to work as my Uncle John's hodder and we got on reasonably well together. Uncle John was a lay preacher - one of those fire and brimstone chaps who always put the fear of God in you. I remember well his views on the subject of swearing. He used to preach to me continuously on the subject and would say, "If I catch thou'st swearing Reg, you get no pocket money and you will burn in Hell."

It was very difficult to control the urge to swear when he was around. If it became unbearable I would try to find a quiet spot out of his earshot and give vent to my frustrations.

I was glad when I became a hodder to Bumps Carpenter a rugby player from Cinderford who played for Gloucester at weekends. I really enjoyed working with him because he was allowed to leave work early on Saturdays to play rugby which meant that I finished work early too. This was on a regular basis which suited me. I would get home early, have a bath and something to eat, jump on my secondhand push-bike and cycle the twelve miles to Gloucester to see my hero play. But the lure of earning an extra shilling (five pence) a week brought my early Saturdays to an end.

I was visiting Grandmother's brother, the wheelwright with the wooden leg, when I met Mr Bennett from Factory Road. We passed the time of day and he asked me how I was getting on at work. One thing led to another and the subject turned to my weekly wage at the colliery.

"Look Reg, if you come to work for me at Crump Meadow Colliery, I'll give you an extra shilling a week."

I jumped at the chance of extra money and started working for Mr Bennett and Mr Baggett.

Mr Bennett was a good boss and he even helped me put on the hodder's harness every morning. Mr Baggett was a miserable man and kept on at me for something or other all the time. Eventually Mr Bennett had a terrible row with him over the way he treated me.

"Leave that boy alone, he is a good worker," Mr Bennett said.

Both men had hazardous jobs as fettlers, inspecting the pit shafts every morning by riding on top of the cage. It was dangerous and dirty work. Rather them than me, I thought.

If six to eight tons were shifted per day they considered that to be a fair day's work and the pay at the end of the week was between eight and nine shillings. Less if we failed to reach the target. Because of Mr Baggett's attitude towards me I did not stay there long. I was sorry to leave Mr Bennett because he had always treated me fairly, but he understood.

I decided to join Dad at the New Fancy.

It was lucky that I had a push-bike because it was a long walk from Cinderford to the New Fancy - a round trip of eight miles. I used to ride the pitch black forest paths on my bike. I was a daredevil but in that spooky atmosphere when a shrieking owl whizzed passed my head my hair stood on end. The greatest hazard were the sheep who would choose to sit across the narrow pathways. I would be cycling along the path when bingo, the bike went one way and I went the other and landed in bracken. At least it was a soft landing. Once again, Dad and I worked as a team at the mine and at the end of the shift I would race home on my bike to prepare the dinner before Dad arrived home. Dad was a stickler for time and liked his meal to be ready when he arrived home. Woe betide me if it wasn't.

As the mornings grew lighter, Dad and I would check on our pigs at Grandfather's place. We would walk along near Victoria Road, passed the furnaces by the Forgehammer pub. On one such morning we came across a most appalling and gruesome sight which stopped us in our tracks. We stood in disbelief as in a small orchard we saw a woman hanging from an apple tree, her toes just four inches above the ground. The weight of her body had pulled the branch downwards. I was too numb to move. Dad went for help and he and several men helped to cut her down. One of the men went to inform the police. By the time our statements were taken the morning was almost over and we arrived late for work that day. My mind was certainly not on work. Neither was

Dad's I'm sure. It was a deeply upsetting experience. When I closed my eyes at night the scene was vivid in my mind and the nightmares stayed with me for a long time. I do not why the poor woman took her life. There was much village gossip and speculation.

One Saturday morning, Dad brought home a new companion called Jack who was to become a permanent member of the family. Jack and Dad became bosom pals and drinking partners. Jack let Dad win every argument. An Irish setter, he had a lovely temperament. He and Dad were inseparable. Jack's knowledge of the local pubs surpassed Dad's in no time.

Man and dog would enter the premises and take a pew. Dad would order a pint for himself then ask the publican, "Thou'st don't mind landlord if the dog has half a pint and a packet of crisps do you?"

"Not in the least," the landlord replied.

As Dad proceeded to enjoy the brew, Jack, lying below him, was lapping his own half pint. They both became quite famous and were the talk of Cinderford, especially when `Time gentlemen please' was called. As Dad and Jack made their way home they used to pass some of the men playing cards on the Green and the usual comment was, "Thou'st can't tell which one is the most sober, Sam or the dog. Sam has to work in the morning, the dog hasn't. As to which one will have the worst hangover is anybody's guess!"

Regardless of what Dad imbibed the night before he would be up for work next morning.

Jack was still out for the count.

With the coming of spring, Uncle Will would bring out his pony and trap. Now that I was older he allowed me to take over the reins. This was usually at weekends when he did his rounds of local pubs in the area. He was always one over the top on these escapades. One particular incident I remember only too well. Uncle Will, worse the wear for drink, put me in charge of his high spirited pony. I was doing quite well or so I thought. We were travelling from Mosel Green towards the Rising Sun. The pony was high stepping and travelling at speed along the road. There was a difference of opinion between me and the pony as to which way we were going and the trap landed on its side in a deep ditch. The sudden jolt woke Uncle Will and in his drunken stupor he called me every name he could think of. Even so he managed to right the trap for the journey home. That was the last time I would ever take the reins. Little did either of us know that poor Uncle Will's life would be cut short a year or so later. He had been to the Ruspidge pub. It was dark and he was walking across a bridge that had no walls either side. He over balanced and fell into the brook below. Dad, realising he was overdue, went out to look for him and found him lying face down in the brook. Uncle Will had landed on a sharp rock which had broken his ribs, which, in turn, had pierced his lungs.

God bless him. He was harmless enough.

My cycling rides through the forest to work were now more pleasurable than winter ones. At least I could see where I was going and avoid those stupid sheep. The splash of colour used to make my mind wander for a minute or two but I had no time to dawdle and I would cycle like hell to get to work on time.

The day started out like any other but this was a day that would alter the entire course of my young life. A very simple and trivial incident became instrumental in my leaving home. I finished the shift at the New Fancy and cycled home to cook dinner. I thought that a rice pudding would do nicely for afters. Everything was under control by the time Dad arrived home. Dad, Edytha, Merlin and I settled down to enjoy the meal, the rice pudding cooking in the oven as we tucked into our main course. We were all looking forward to the rice pudding. As I started to remove it from the oven I noticed I had burnt the top of the pudding. Dad played hell. One word led to another and I decided to leave home there and then.

"If thou goes through that door, you won't come back," he said.

"Don't worry, I won't," I replied.

I went upstairs and packed what few belongings I possessed and off I went, leaving Edytha and Merlin with bewildered looks on their faces.

Where I was going, I had no idea, but I was determined that I would not go back.

Where shall I go? What shall I do? I thought.

I wandered around Cinderford for a while and then went to my favourite refuge in times of trouble - the forest. The tears flowed. I cried for Mam, the only one who ever showed me any affection. I wanted to die. Dad did not love me. He never showed me any affection. All I got from him were dictatorial demands and hidings. I did not care whether I lived or died. My shirt was wet with tears. I was alone. Completely alone. Nobody wanted me. Nobody cared. Only Mam and she wasn't here.

When there were no tears left, I pondered as to what I should do.

I'll go to Gloucester, that's what I'll do and join the army. At least I would get three square meals a day and clothes for my back.

13 - *Joining Up*

The decision made, I got on my bicycle and headed for Gloucester via Littledean and Westbury-on-Severn.

At fifteen I was too young to enlist but this did not deter me. I lied about my age to the army recruiting officer. He tried to persuade me to join the Gloucester Regiment but I was adamant. I wanted to join the Wiltshire Regiment because I liked their regimental badge.

From Gloucester I travelled by train to Bristol where I spent the next few days at Horfield Barracks before being transferred to Reading to join the Royal Berkshire Regiment, the army's choice for me.

During the next few months I began to settle into the regimental way of life: preparing my kit for inspection, rifle drill, guard duty and the hardest of all - square bashing. The meals were regular. That was the main thing.

Everything was going smoothly until one morning I was told to go and see the Commanding Officer. I sat down and waited to be called in, wondering why he wanted to see me. I straightened myself up, knocked on the door, waited for the command and walked in saluting.

The Commanding Officer looked very serious as he said to me, "Private Morgan, you lied about your age."

"Yes, sir," was all that I could reply.

They say your sins will find you out and that was the case for me. I received a severe reprimand for deceiving army authorities and my discharge papers were prepared and handed to me the next morning, together with my fare home.

The last words uttered to me as I was leaving were, "Come back in twelve months' time."

I had plenty of time to think during the journey back to Cinderford and I decided to visit my grandmother's sister, Aunty Nell. I explained what had happened and knowing the family situation, God love her, she took me in. Aunty Nell had children of her own: Robert, Sam, Bill, Bessy, Mary, Lucy, Alice and Albert. She had a heart of gold, Aunty Nell. I had to share a bed with Bill and he became like a brother to me, although I missed Merlin and Edytha, with whom I had no contact.

My first priority was to find employment so I could pay my way. I could not go back to the New Fancy because Dad was still working there so I tried my luck at the Eastern United Colliery. This colliery was a drift mine. There would be no hodding, thank goodness. At least in some places I could stand upright and I thought that I was in clover. There was no cage and I entered the mine by sitting in a trolley travelling down the incline towards the first landing stage. On arrival I transferred with the other miners from the trolley to a second group of trolleys down another incline which led to the final landing stage. It was then a one or two mile walk to the coal face. Once again, medium sized ponies were employed to ferry the full and empty trams into the lay-by. Like the men they worked damn hard.

Two of Aunty Nell's sons had nasty accidents at this mine. Sam suffered an injury to his back which forced a change of job from miner to weigh man. He was responsible for weighing the loaded trams on a scale to assess tonnage. Albert,the youngest, suffered an horrific accident. His face was badly smashed up and he had to undergo complete reconstruction but he was never the same again. The pain and agony he suffered must have been terrible. He was never to fully recover. Eventually, Albert left the Forest to settle in Wales at Merthyr Tydfil, Mid Glamorgan. But things began to go downhill for him. He became an alcoholic and took his own life. Poor soul.

Bill, his brother, worked at Lightmoor Colliery as a hodder for his father and being tall must have found it hard to work in such conditions. Although Bill and I became bosom pals, we did not share the same interests. Bill's great passion was woodwork and he would spend most evenings reading books on the subject.

"Come to the cinema, Bill?" I would ask.

"No, Reg, I want to read my book," he would reply.

"See you later then," and off I would go.

What did I want with books, I thought. I've learned more out of school than when I was there. I wasn't meant to be a bookworm. Like most young people I lacked foresight and lived for the present. The future was miles away. Whilst I lived the fantasies projected on the cinema screen, Bill would be sitting in the chair with his head in his interesting book. He would still be there when I returned home. All that study certainly paid off in Bill's case. Like me, Bill loathed the mines.

"Surely, Reg, there must be better ways of earning a living," he would say.

Eventually he decided to leave the Forest mines forever. I remember the humble beginnings of his now successful business which he has left in the capable hands of his widow, Kath and their three sons. Bill purchased a foot treadle lathe and started on a small scale to turn out legs for tables and chairs. He did his utmost to persuade me to become a partner. I felt that if I accepted his offer I would offend his elder brother, Sam. So I declined. Bill had a wonderful talent and knowledge of wood which he passed on to his sons who still trade under the name T.W. Bonser, Joiner, Church Road, Cinderford. If you want quality and craftsmanship, look no further.

While Bill was busy setting up his business, I was slogging hard in the mines, happy in the knowledge that I had a roof over my head and people who cared for me. As long as I could pay my way I was content. Transport was my main priority as the buses were infrequent and pedal power was needed. I saved hard to purchase another bicycle. Apart from the odd puncture or two that means of travel did not cost me a penny and gave me great pleasure and independence.

Saturday was my favourite cycling day. Sometimes I would ride to Ross-on-Wye, Gloucester or even to Dursley to visit Alice, Aunty Nell's married daughter.

The main social events of the summer were Barton Fair in July and the eagerly anticipated August annual outing to Weston-super-Mare from the Colliers Arms pub, Cinderford. Barton Fair was held just outside the City of Gloucester and it was a big day for everyone.

To the local farmers it was a business Fair where wheeling and dealing over livestock took the best part of the day. Buyer and seller each tried to obtain the best deal possible. The bargaining antics were an entertainment in themselves. There was no written agreement, just verbal exchanges and a slapping of each other's hands when a deal was struck. There were looks of great satisfaction as buyer proudly showed off his latest acquisition and seller held a fistful of notes and smiled ear to ear.

The children were more interested in the animals. The Gypsies were excellent judges of horse flesh and brought their best mounts to be auctioned off. They drove a hard bargain but usually got what they wanted in the end. To the working man it was an excuse for an all day boozing party free from the wife and kids. The poor mothers struggled with three or four over-excited children all clamouring for rides on various carousels and asking for pennies for the sideshows. As far as the men were concerned, the women were having a whale of a time.

Grabbing a bite of lunch along the way, I spent the day wandering around, soaking in the atmosphere of the Fair. Come evening I cycled home and related to Aunty Nell all that I had seen and heard.

Sleep did not come easily but the next day was Sunday and a day of rest. I believed in a Creator but had no inclination to attend church or chapel. As a young lad I had better things to do with my spare time. From what I had heard, chapel rules and regulations were too restrictive for my liking. However, I did possess two qualities that were acceptable to the Ladies Temperance Movement: abstinence from drinking and smoking. Later I did occasionally go to chapel on a dull Sunday evening, wearing my one decent outfit. I enjoyed the service, at least the parts that I listened to. My mind tended to wander until the singing brought me back to earth. I thought the sermon endless and the wooden benches so uncomfortable. I would be out of the door as soon as the service ended, back to Aunty Nell's to change my clothes. Best clothes had to be looked after. I still change my clothes as soon as I arrive home.

Sometimes whilst out walking on Sunday I hoped by chance to catch a glimpse of Merlin and Edytha but it never happened. Occasionally I did bump into other relatives: Uncle George or my cousins. Uncle George was thrifty and was continually trying to find new hiding places to stash his savings from my Aunt who was excellent at discovering money. Uncle was famous for his prize cabbages and thought that he had found the ideal place to hide his cash. His cabbages were his pride and joy and no one was allowed near them. He told my Aunt not to cut the cabbages, he would attend to that himself. However, he did this once too often and aroused her suspicions. When his back was turned, his hiding place was discovered. Uncle George tried dry stone walls, the coal shed, the toilet and even under the flagged floor, but like the bloodhound she was Aunt found every hiding place. It is a pity Uncle didn't put his savings in the bank. At least he would have had sight of his money again.

Although I considered myself a bit of a loner, I sometimes craved companionship with my mates. We arranged to meet at a spot in the forest, each carrying a piece of cheese, bread and a raw onion in a bag. We would spend many a pleasant hour walking through the forest and there was always a new pathway to explore. The dense, eerie atmosphere triggered off stories of ghosts and murders and we tried to be out of the forest before darkness fell. One particular night I said goodbye to my mates and walked along past Foxes Bridge Colliery a little later than usual. On the path I met a local girl, a distant relation of mine, heading the same way. It was a moonlit night and together we walked along the path. Suddenly, an apparition appeared to be floating up and down ahead of us. We stopped dead in our tracks and froze, too scared to move. We could not go back because this was the only way home. Finally, plucking up courage, I grabbed her hand and we ran like the devil past the apparition.

What a relief when we realised that the `apparition' was a white goat reaching up a tree to strip off bark. We saw the funny side of it and could not stop laughing all the way home.

Living in close proximity to the River Wye, famous for its salmon, I not only knew about the poaching but took part. Most Foresters knew of this activity, but turned a blind eye. The more experienced lads knew that the best pickings were at Lower Lydbrook. We went to the river at nightfall and set up a tent for shelter. Then we lit carbon lamps and sat along the river's edge. The light from our lamps dazzled the salmon as they slept near the river bank, allowing us to spear them. It was a risky business. If someone fell in the river he was on his own. Your friends would not be able to find you in the dark. The other danger was being caught by river patrols which meant a brush with the law and a criminal record. In those days the police were feared. I was no angel but I made up my mind not to be led astray by the older lads again.

I must admit, though, that I enjoyed my portion of salmon.

A wet day in Cinderford could be pretty miserable. I would sometimes wander around window shopping to try to keep from under Aunty Nell's feet for a while. If I was lucky I would bump into my friends, like the Beddis boys, and they would take me to their home for an hour or two. I felt a little uncomfortable being unable to return their invitation.

The Beddis family were decent folk and Mrs Beddis was a young widow whose husband had died at the early age of thirty six. He was a miner yet his death was due to natural causes. Whilst working underground he collapsed and died. Mrs Beddis was left with a family of four children, three boys and one girl named Hilda. Mrs Beddis's life was one constant struggle yet she coped very well. She was a hard working lady and her daughter Hilda was the same. On some occasions I declined their invitation to visit because I did not want to impose myself upon them for all their kindness.

On some weekends I used to visit relatives in Foxes Bridge and occasionally my path would cross Hilda's as she was going in the same direction to visit her relations. We would then take the shortcut through the forest which saved us several miles.

Aunty Nell and my adopted family did their best to make my seventeenth birthday a happy day. I did not receive cards from my family and I had a great sense of loneliness. Past memories came flooding back to haunt me: the good memories and the bad, which I tried to blot out. I was glad when the day was over. It's no good looking back all the time, Reg, I told myself, you have to go forward and get on with your life. I had steady employment and a regular wage and after I had paid my dues I still had enough money left to save for the annual trip to the seaside. Like everyone who was planning to go I paid a few pence a week to the landlord of the Colliers Arms, Cinderford who was elected fund holder for the outing. He was head cook and bottle washer with several dogsbodies running here and there organising things. The hope was that on the day everything would run smoothly. This time there was to be no charabanc. We were to travel in style by means of that wonderful invention, the steam locomotive.

The trip was always arranged during the school holidays for the children's benefit and they just could not wait for the summer term to end. Although it was still several weeks away, the trip to Weston-super-Mare was the main topic of conversation throughout Cinderford. The draper's shop was almost out of thread and material. Needles in hand the women frantically tried to complete their summer dresses and children's clothes for the trip, although very often the mended old dress or suit had to do.

The most important item for the men was the organisation of the booze. If that was overlooked and left behind it would be a catastrophe.

The night before would find the children having their weekly bath in front of the fire under mother's supervision. As one stepped out, the next stepped in. Bath night was not popular. Clothes were laid out ready for the next morning. Sandwiches and cakes had to be prepared and packed ready for the trip.

It was an early start for everyone as we made our way to Cinderford Station. The men wore their best bib and tucker. The women looked pretty in their new or nearly new outfits as they struggled with heavy eyed children and carried food supplies. There was great excitement amongst the older children as most had never been on a train before. The silent plea was, Please let it be fine.

"The train's coming," was the cry.

Everyone safely on board, the train proceeded on its way to the City of Gloucester. On arrival we were greeted by, "All change for Weston-super-Mare."

Parents ensured that no child was left behind then we settled into another train whilst the men ensured that the crates of beer had not been forgotten.

Green flag up, whistle blown and we were off at last. The excited chatter on board the train was deafening at times but who could complain. It was such a special day and we were all determined to enjoy it. Sunshine, sea and sand was the order of the day, except for the menfolk with their greater interest in liquid refreshments. The children were impatient and fidgeted continually, asking, "Are we there yet, Mam?" I was content, looking out through the window at the beautiful scenery as the train sped towards the sea.

By the time we arrived the picnic had already begun. The way the children scoffed sandwiches it was surprising that there were any left for the rest of the day. After what seemed a long walk we finally reached the front. But there was no sign of the sea.

"It's out there," someone shouted.

The tide was out. How disappointing. However, there was plenty of sand for the bucket and spade mob and they soon got over the initial shock. There was always the good old Punch and Judy show and the donkeys rides as well as ice creams all round and plenty of tea. The wind was getting up and sand got into everything. Even the sandwiches were gritty but who cared about the odd grain of sand if you were hungry.

I was determined to find the sea.

I was doing well until I reached mud. Have you ever tried walking through thick, black, slimy mud in your bare feet? Undeterred, I plodded on for what seemed several miles. I had always imagined the sea to be clear and blue but it was dirty and looked like a muddy wallow for pigs. Was that it, after trudging all this way?

It was ages before I reached clean sand again and it stuck to the mud on my feet. I hated the sand between my toes but had to grin and bear it until I got to the children's small sea water pool to wash it off and get my shoes and socks on. It was time for me to explore the promenade. I walked along the front to the old pier away from the town. It was a pleasant walk, ice cream in hand. I sat down to enjoy the bracing sea air. Time was moving on. I made my way through the town just window shopping as money was short. Not having a watch I hoped that the town clock was correct and I did not venture too far because the train was leaving at 5.30 PM. As I made my way to the station I met up with my travelling companions who looked tired out, especially the women and children. The men were drifting back in dribs and drabs having had a wonderful time within the confines of the four walls of the local pubs.

I doubt if any of them had seen anything of Weston-super-Mare!

We all hoped that no one was left behind as we clambered aboard the train. The women and children were quiet and it was the merry men who disrupted the children's slumber as we journeyed home, singing the usual songs like *Ten Green Bottles*. The children managed to sleep through it until they were aroused at Gloucester to change trains. It was almost dark by the time we arrived at Cinderford Station. We walked home together and gradually grew fewer as each family reached their front door. Goodnights said, they disappeared inside. I had thoroughly enjoyed myself but was glad to get home. Soon it was nothing but a pleasant memory, but one that lived in the children's minds forever.

Who knew when their parents could afford to go again?

The mine owners were having financial difficulties and imposed a reduction in the working week from five to four days, then three. By autumn we were working only one or two days. Our wages were drastically reduced. I did not have enough money to pay my keep. Aunty Nell was a kind-hearted person but I felt terrible that I could not pay my way and started to look for alternative work.

At Dursley a new firm called Listers was starting up business making machinery. I went as far as arranging an interview for the following Monday morning. But I was filled with misgivings as mining was the only work I knew.

Perhaps I would not fit in. If I failed, where I would be then?

I could not impose upon Aunty Nell's generosity any longer. Life was tough enough for her already. I did not want to leave the Forest. It was my home. It was a hard decision but I determined to go back to Grandmother's in Cefn Fforest (Garden City) and get a job doing the work I knew.

14 - *From Forest to Cefn Fforest*

It was late October, 1928 when I said my fond farewells to Aunty Nell, Bill and the family. We were all sad. Once again I was leaving my beloved Forest, not realising that this time it would be forever.

Dressed against the cold, I packed my few possessions into my saddle bag, together with the sandwiches Aunty Nell had kindly given me.

It would take several hours to cycle to Grandmother's home and she had no idea I was coming because my decision had been made on impulse. Besides, I would arrive before a letter.

The first part of my journey was downhill towards Monmouth, then I followed the road leading to Pontypool, legs aching like hell by the time I reached Grandmother's front door.

"Reg! What are you doing here?" she exclaimed.

It did not take me long to explain my situation to Grandmother and Grandfather and they listened intently.

"You can stay here, Reg. At least until something comes along," Grandfather said.

I could not thank them enough.

Monday morning arrived and as I awoke I wondered where I was. Then I realised I was in Wales and that my first priority was to find employment. My first port of call was the Gelli Level where Dad and had I worked until Mam's untimely death in 1925. I had more confidence now. As I approached the manager's office I felt I had the necessary experience to back me up.

The interview went well and the manager decided to employ me.

"When can you start?" he asked.

"Immediately, sir!" I replied.

Six days a week and a regular wage. I was in clover. I did not intend to take up the bad habits of smoking or drinking. I had seen what they led to with my own eyes. With extra money in my pocket I would be able to save up for my one and only true love. A motorbike.

A push-bike was alright. But a motorbike would be heaven.

The tools required by every miner were, a pick for digging out the coal, a shovel for filling the trams, an axe for cutting the timber supports and a sledgehammer for driving in the steel wedge to break the coal into sizable pieces. In an eight hour shift four or five trams were filled per day. Once again, the horse was a work mate, taking the full trams from the coal face to the mouth of the level. The trams were placed one by one in a tumbler and by the application of the lever, the tumbler would revolve and the coal in the now upside down tram was tipped into the railway wagons lined up outside for transportation to the main railway line.

Wages were determined by the number of trams you filled during the week. Each tram was marked with chalk so the weigher could register how many trams you filled by your initials. The more trams you filled, the more money you got. It was gruelling work, but I was used to hard work in the Forest mines.

It was very wet at this level because it was near the surface. Water flowed like a brook. We worked on a rise so the water drained away from us and there was no need for pumps.

I felt sorry for the women. Every day the men came home soaking wet. Then it was the old dolly tub and scrubbing board. No modern luxuries like a washing machine or spin drier. The clothes had to be dried in front of the fire for the next day.

In this mine there was no fear of an explosion because there was no fear of gas. Naked lights and carbide lamps were used. You could even smoke at the coalface. There was more head-room for man and horse. You could even stand up straight.

It was hard graft. I was always glad when the shift ended. During the week I had to go to bed early because I had to be up by six the next morning.

The horses worked as hard as the miners and I was happy that the horses were allowed to leave the mine every night. They did not of course receive a pay packet at the end of the week, but green fields and fresh hay might have been some reward. The horses were partial to a juicy apple, a carrot or a cabbage which the miners often brought them and they would even search the men's pockets with their noses looking for their treat.

At the weekend I used to walk to where the horses grazed just to enjoy the sight of them galloping across the meadow kicking their legs in the air as if to unseat a rider. I wondered what was on their minds when they had to go down the mine again the next day. Probably the same thoughts each miner had, Another day's hard slog.

Mr. Munn, the owner of Gelli Level, was satisfied with my work and I began to settle in well. With the family around me, I did not feel so alone.

For the next few weeks I remained at my grandmother's. Finally, Aunt Sophia, Mam's sister, invited me to lodge at her home in Davies Street. Not wanting to impose on my grandmother, I accepted and moved in with Aunt Sophia and Uncle Jack, the war hero, who was a miner at Oakdale Colliery.

Uncle Jack was a Police Special, so I had to watch my p's and q's.

It was three and a half years since Mam's passing and the pain was still there. Tears stung my eyes that Christmas as I stood at her grave-side, a piece of holly between my fingers. The long walk to Bedwellty Church was traumatic for me and the memories came flooding back. I missed my mam and my spirits were low as the December air chilled my bones.

Each week I placed half a crown, two shillings and six pence (twelve and a half pence) in the motorbike jar on my chest of drawers. I soon realised, however, that something very strange was happening. The half crown was mysteriously transformed into a florin, two shilling (ten pence). This was most puzzling. I even began to question whether I had made a mistake myself. I was sure I had placed half a crown in my jar. The same thing went on for several weeks. The half crown I had saved on Friday was by Monday a florin.

Eventually, I found out who the culprit was.

Uncle Jack!

His poison was gambling. Cards. My sixpence was his stake.

What could I do about it?

They gave me a roof over my head and a bed to lie on. And I was part of the family.

I decided to turn a blind eye for the time being. One day the answer came to me in a flash. I would put a florin in the jar instead of a half crown.

Believe it or not, that did the trick. When Uncle Jack realised I was onto him, he laughed and gave me a `good for you' wink.

Uncle Jack and I got on very well together. He would talk to me about his experiences in the First World War, mostly the comical incidents, which were few and far between. We spent many winter evenings at the fireside putting the world to rights whilst Aunt Sophia struggled with the chores. Sometimes I would play the mouth organ and Uncle Jack and his gambling pals would have a good old singsong, until it was time to get the cards out. The game went on long after I had gone to bed at ten o'clock, sometimes until the early hours.

Why shouldn't he have fun after what he'd been through in the war? I often thought.

The tide was beginning to turn for the women of Aunt Sophia's generation. It was a pity Mam did not live to see this period of emancipation. Women over the age of twenty one finally achieved the vote in 1928.

Having lived through the hardships and deprivations suffered by us, the working classes, I was aware it was a question of them and us, the owners of the mines and the miners. It was here in South Wales that I finally began to understand and take an interest in politics. Dad's generation had struggled for years to have a reasonable living wage and a decent standard of living. Why should the privileged few have it all?

My Mother, Kate Amelia, and me

My Wife, Phyllis

My Father and Jack

Sarah Ellen and Owen
holding Phyllis

Brian and Elaine

Phyllis and Brian

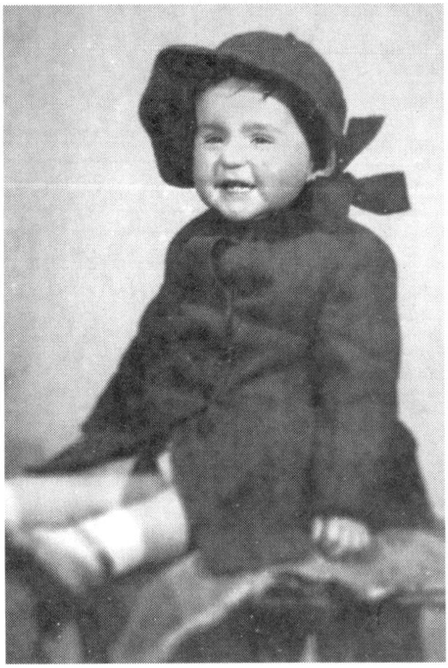

Elaine

With the Pioneer Corps

Egypt

Phyllis and me

Kate Amelia

Merlin

Me holding Elaine

Brian

Egypt

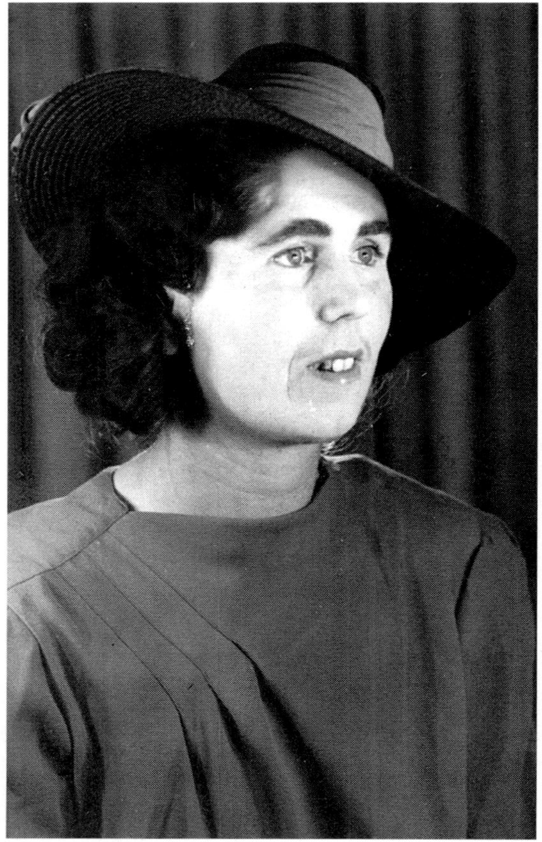

Phyllis

Merlin and me

An Old Soldier

We were decent folk asking for fair play. That is all.

Here in South Wales our saviour was the Labour Party. We backed it to the hilt.

By 16th April, 1929, my eighteenth birthday, things began to take a turn for the worse. Abroad, Welsh coal was no longer in heavy demand. Other countries were now mining their own coal successfully. In mining communities throughout the country, unemployment began to rise at an alarming rate. I realised how lucky I was to have a job at Gelli Level. But one particular day I thought I was going to lose my job.

Whilst working in the main heading road, my sixth sense warned me that something was wrong. I began to run. Suddenly, the whole roof fell in behind me. When I felt it was safe to surface I scrambled back to the main heading. On the spot where I had been working, the sun was now shining. I could see the blue sky above.

A report was made to the manager and he came to inspect the damage. I took a deep breath. I was sure I was for the push. But I kept my job. The manager thought it was the best thing that could have happened. The men now had a second escape route to the surface and more fresh air.

"You've saved me some money lad. Be certain to shore it up with stout timber," he said.

Thank goodness he was an understanding man. It could have easily gone the other way. The fear of losing your job was always at the back of your mind.

I was eighteen years old and on the threshold of life, but not master of my own fate. Hard work never killed anyone, but it could certainly destroy the soul. I lived, slept and ate work. It did, however, bring me closer to my dream of owning a motor-bike.

In my leisure time I found that my pals were beginning to drift away, beginning to build their own lives. Their interests were in the shape of the female form. At that time I was not interested in girls, or settling down. I felt I wanted to travel and see the world.

The Rhymney Valley League Football Association consisted of all the local mines in the area and miners formed the bulk of the teams. My Uncle Percy was a keen player and persuaded me to join his team, Cefn Fforest. I was looking forward to my first match against Bedlinog, playing right wing with Uncle Percy as centre forward. But where were the other players? We eventually found them in a pub, half cut. Unsurprisingly we were clobbered, ten nil. From then on I became spectator rather than player.

Uncle Jack spurred me on and I finally became the proud owner of a second hand Douglas belt drive with a flat petrol tank.

What a beauty!

Little did I realise how many British bikes I would own over the next decade and how many thrills and spills I would have on the A.J.S., the Velocette which was a really fast machine, the Cotton, Norton, Rudge, B.S.A., Matchless, Triumph, Ariel and the Royal Enfield.

With the Douglas, life took on a new meaning for me. Things went well for a while until the belt broke several times. I decided that enough was enough. I wanted a more reliable machine. The A.J.S., 350cc, chain driven was the answer. Changing gear was a lot easier than it had been on the Douglas and it was a real pleasure to ride.

At the weekend the roads were virtually free of traffic. I rode through the Cotswolds, Oxfordshire and Worcestershire. On these runs I really put the bike through her paces. It is strange how youth has a passion for speed. I was no different.

On one outing I failed to negotiate a tight bend and went straight through a hedge and landed upside-down in a field full of cows. They stared back at me with their big brown eyes and continued chewing the cud.

Some animals are not easy to impress, whatever you do.

Sometimes Uncle Jack came with me and we visited several of his relatives, including some at Radnor. Their home was beautiful and they seemed to me real gentry. I proceeded to enjoy the tea, with my best airs and graces, and things were going well until I ever so carefully sliced the pickled onion with my knife and it catapulted across the table into our host's cup of tea. They did not bat an eyelid, but I was mortified. Uncle Jack never let me forget that incident.

When money was short I could not afford petrol and then I used to go for long walks, revisiting haunts of my childhood. Nothing much had altered. Toff Bond was still sitting on his stool outside his front door. He was a real character. Sunday mornings would find him sitting there in his best bib and tucker which stuck out a mile because his trousers and jacket were the same old shabby outfit he had worn all week. Sunday was Sunday to Toff and it was his way of making an effort to look tidy. Hence the nickname.

My Uncle Harry was courting Toff's daughter, his only child. One child was enough for Mrs Bond to cope with, poor woman. Grandfather from Pwllglas used to frequent the same pub as Toff and knew him and his family well. When Grandfather knew of Harry's fancy for the girl he never ceased to pull Uncle Harry's leg about the situation.

"Surely you can do better than that Harry," Grandfather retorted.

When going to visit his girlfriend, Uncle Harry would spend ages sprucing himself up. Grandfather never understood why. Uncle Harry would arrive at the front door of the house which looked respectable from the outside but as soon as the door opened a regiment of chickens would march out. Uncle Harry, dressed in his Sunday best, would be politely offered a chair whilst Toff and his Missis were finishing their dinner. The scraps that fell from the table were gobbled up by the chickens who had the complete run of the house. We could not understand how he could sit there amongst it all but they do say that love is blind.

Eventually, Uncle Harry finally got the message and knitted up with another lass more to Grandfather's liking. Yet she turned out to be one of the biggest working class snobs of all times.

Her comment to Edytha in later years was, "You do realise, Edytha, that I married beneath my station."

Poor Uncle Harry was to suffer a very bad accident at Britannia Colliery (at that time I was a deputy at the colliery) in later years, bringing his mining career to an end. A big stone fell on him and badly damaged his legs and pelvis. Yet he considered himself lucky and did eventually recover with the help of his wife and two sons. He also managed to obtain light work outside the industry but was restricted as a result of his injuries.

In the mining valleys of South Wales, especially the Rhondda, Rhymney and Aberdare valleys, things began to go steadily downhill. The situation was pretty desperate. Coal was no longer king and the mining communities of these valleys, totally dependent on the coal industry, began to feel the effects of rising unemployment as mines closed. There was no alternative employment to fall back on, only the degradation of the dole queue, the parish (if you were lucky enough to get anything), or the indignity of the means test. A sense of guilt overwhelmed because I had a job while thousands of miners with large families to support were unemployed. I was single and only had to look after myself.

With the closure of the Ebbw Vale Steel Works and the mighty Wall Street crash in October 1929, the mining communities of South Wales prepared themselves for the big crunch. The dark days of the Depression had arrived with a vengeance. It was time to pull in the belt still tighter. There was no foreseeable way out.

Once again, Welsh miners were struggling for their very survival.

Christmas 1929 would be truly Dickensian for the unemployed and downtrodden working classes of the South Wales valleys. Miners' children with noses pressed hard against the frosted parlour panes of the well-to-do, watched coal owners' families enjoying all the thrills and delights that came with Christmas. Owners may have been out of pocket but that was nothing compared to the mining communities' sufferings and hardship.

I did not know what 1930 would bring but was certain that things were going to get worse.

15 - *Pochin Deep Mine*

The 1930s were the years of my great passion for the motorbike, the struggles of the working class, my privilege in working alongside one of the famous sons of Wales and meeting my future dear wife Phyllis.

On New Year's Day 1930 there was little cause for celebration. The privately owned Gelli Level was still in production and my job was secure for the time being. If I had been working in one of the deep mines I would have joined the ranks of the unemployed. I felt for those men but there was nothing I could do.

When would it be my turn?

I had lost all contact with my family in Cinderford but Edytha and Merlin were always in my thoughts. I wondered how they were coping living with Dad. I was free from his domination and happier for it.

Yet I wished things could have been different.

I envied some of my friends who had a real family life. I longed for someone to put an arm around me and tell me they loved me.

Merlin would be eight in April and Edytha fifteen in June. As the weeks and months passed I missed them more and more. February was a miserable month. Soon the March winds were blowing the winter cobwebs away. When British Summertime finally arrived I got my motorbike out. I loved the lighter nights and I was determined to make full use of them.

My first expedition was a trip to Uncle Jack's sister in Stourbridge. Both Jack and I had been looking forward to it for weeks. Several members of his family were employed at the famous Stuart Crystal Glassworks and over the years had accumulated a fair collection of beautiful crystal ornaments.

Uncle Jack's family gave us a tremendous welcome and took us to as many places of interest as we could fit in during the weekend. In Stourbridge the unemployment seemed not to be so bad. They could not believe it when we told them about the terrible conditions the mining communities were suffering in South Wales.

"Why don't you come to live up here," they asked.

For a single chap like myself it would have been relatively easy, but Uncle Jack had a home and a family to consider.

A few weeks later Uncle Jack and Aunt Sophia took in another lodger. To my delight it was my sister Edytha. She had had enough of the way Dad behaved. It must have been difficult for her to desert our brother Merlin. This was the second upheaval in his short life. He must have shed a tear under the bedclothes at night. The fact that Edytha had left home proved to me that my departure was not my fault. We understood each other better because of our shared experience.

Until Edytha could find employment I provided for her financially.

The house was crowded but things went well until Edytha was hit by a car in Blackwood. The main thing was that she was alive, but her eyesight was affected. She was told she would have to wear spectacles for the rest of her life. I bought her the first pair. It was both a sad and a proud moment for me.

Unemployment was continuing to rise. Edytha finally decided to move to Hereford to work in domestic service. I really felt for her having to `live in' amongst strangers. It was too far for her to come home at weekends. She worked long hours for little pay with perhaps half a day off, if she was lucky. Exploitation was the name of the game. I wonder sometimes how much has changed.

Fortunately, I was able to visit Edytha on my motorbike. I enjoyed walking around the market town and it reminded me of my childhood days in the Forest. They certainly grew good fruit in that area and I usually took a bag or two home with me.

On rare occasions Edytha was able to come home for the weekend. For a few hours I felt part of a family again. One particular time I brought her home and was travelling at great speed along the country roads towards the Welsh Borders, the wind whistling in my ears. Edytha was clinging on for dear life and trying to hold on to her beret. As we approached a bend she began to shout but I was oblivious to her cries. Apparently a gust of wind had swept her beret from her head. Poor Edytha looked very windswept when we eventually arrived home and grieved for the loss of the beret. I really should have bought her a new one.

Christmas that year was a little subdued for Edytha and I as our thoughts were with Merlin. How we wished things had turned out differently.

After Christmas it was back to the grindstone. Conditions in the Welsh valleys were not improving. There were rumours that the coal seam in the Gelli Level was almost exhausted. Many miners were trying to find employment in other areas. Villages took on a ghost like quality as whole families moved out.

Gone were the youthful voices of the village choir. We Welsh were proud of our musical heritage which had brought us through many a crisis, uplifting our downtrodden spirits in time of need and want. I loved *Cwm Rhondda* and *Myfanwy* (a love song) as much as any Welsh speaker, even though I could not understand one word of the language myself. English was my language because my parents were Foresters, yet they never regarded themselves as English or

Welsh. The Foresters were a breed of their own. I was born in Monmouthshire, yet have always considered myself an English speaking Welshman.

I did not want to leave Wales. I worked and waited and hoped.

Finally the coal seam at Gelli Level did peter out. Mr Munn, the owner, broke the news to us. He was a decent man and I believe he had done his best.

The rapport and comradeship which had been built up between the men over the years vanished like the coal. It was every man for himself.

I did not relish being on the dole so I tried to find work in the deep mines of Pochin and the New Pits near Tredegar and Ebbw Vale.

Deep mining was new to me, but once a miner always a miner.

I eventually found work at Pochin Colliery. It was here that I experienced the dusty conditions that cause pneumoconiosis. Many miners suffered chest problems which, in some cases, led to an early death.

At Pochin there was gas in the mine and there had been two previous explosions resulting in many fatalities. No naked flames were allowed. The men carried locked oil lamps in sealed casing. Every nook and cranny was tested for gas before work could begin.

16 - *Aneurin Bevan*

It was in this mine I had the privilege of working alongside Aneurin Bevan who was later to become a Member of Parliament and founder of the National Health Service. He was a miner like myself and knew from experience of the poverty and hardship within the mining communities. He was also keenly interested in political life, especially the worrying things which were happening in Germany at that time. As young as I was, I realised Aneurin was destined for higher things.

He condemned the exploitation of the working class by the mine owners. The average day's quota was for each man to fill five or six trams with coal. Aneurin and the young lad with him filled one and a half trams per day.

"Why only one and a half trams Aneurin?" I asked one day.

"One tram for me and half for the lad is sufficient work to pay our wages," he replied.

After a few months the owners decided to lay off one shift and I was out on my ear. I missed my many conversations with Aneurin. He taught me a great deal about world affairs. It was a political education you might say and I followed his career intently.

I wore out some shoe leather during the next few weeks searching for work, but to no avail. I had to get some money somehow, so I made a wooden trolley, attached a harness to it and became a human horse again.

Many others had the same idea. It was against the law and if you got caught you were in deep trouble. I used to drag the trolley to Aberbargoed coal tip and it was back breaking work trying to find the best pieces of coal amongst all the waste. But I was not the only one trying to make enough to feed myself. It took several hours to fill the trolley, then the coal was transferred to small sacks. On the way home I sold the coal for one shilling and sixpence (seven and a half pence) a bag.

For several months I tried to earn a shilling or two the best way I could. Chopping wood, tidying up peoples gardens and collecting firewood, that's how I spent my days.

I thought I would never find work. Of course, I was not alone.

I heard that there was the chance of work further down the valley at Bedwas Colliery. I crossed my fingers and prayed. My prayers paid off. Bedwas Colliery was ten miles from home. This meant a very early start in the mornings.

But a job was a job.

This mine was a different kettle of fish and I had to walk several miles underground before I reached the coalface. It was steep and I was exhausted before I even started work. There were no horses in this mine, everything was mechanised.

Each miner used a coal pick powered by compressed air and this was a great improvement on the pickaxe. At the coalface there were twenty men working as a team. The noise from the coal picks was deafening. A conveyor belt transported the coal to the waiting trams by means of a Holman engine, again powered by compressed air. The trams were moved from pit bottom to pit top by cage. From there the coal was tipped into railway trucks for transportation to Cardiff and Barry Docks for shipment abroad.

The owners decided to purchase a coal cutter to extract coal more quickly. The coal seam was four and a half feet thick and ran along the face for one hundred and thirty yards. As the machine cut the coal, wooden blocks were placed underneath the coal to support it and keep it stable. The roof was shored up with wooden blocks until the morning shift arrived. The coal had to be cleared away before the end of the morning shift and timbers were again used to support the roof. The cutterman needed space to travel the face so a track was prepared while the machine was in operation to prevent timbers from being knocked out as he made his way along the face. The afternoon shift was responsible for cutting the coal and the morning shift was responsible for clearing it away. This meant four to five hundred trams could be filled per shift. It was a mad house.

At the pithead there were baths so at least I was able to wash off the coal dust and sweat and put on clean dry clothes. We welcomed this luxury greatly, though the women still had to wash the dirty clothes the men brought home.

At this time I struck up a relationship with a local girl who was still at grammar school. Her name was Morfydd Lewis. She came from a talented musical family. Her father was the organist at the chapel and the conductor of the local choir. Morfydd's brother Richard had been trained to sing by his father and was a fine baritone. Richard won a prestigious place at Covent Garden.

Another Welsh voice lost from the valleys.

Morfydd encouraged me to take an interest in music and I joined the chapel choir. This was more to impress her father than anything else. She was pushing me far too fast. I did not like Morfydd telling me what to do and who to impress, so I ended the relationship.

Besides, I was not ready to settle down just yet.

For a while I blotted girls out of my mind and concentrated on the motorbike once more. I enjoyed cleaning and maintaining it. I was determined not to get involved with another girl for a long time.

Famous last words.

17 - *An Eventful Year*

In mid-January, 1935, cupid's arrow found its mark. Love came in the form of a dark haired, fair skinned, blue eyed beauty. Her name was Phyllis and she was gorgeous. She was the typical English rose, though she was Welsh and proud of it.

Our first meeting was at the local fish shop. She had a box of matches in her hand and I offered to carry it for her. What a stupid way to get to talk to her. But it worked. As we walked along the street I asked her for a date and to my surprise she said yes.

I cannot remember where we went on our first date but I knew it would not be the last.

There were rivals for her affection, but I think my motorbike impressed her as not everyone had transport in those days and we took occasional trips into the countryside. Her father was very strict and Phyllis had to be home by a certain time or there would be hell to play. One particular day we had travelled a considerable distance on the bike and as I dropped her off and raced off, poor Phyllis was left sitting in the middle of the road shouting after me. Her legs, numb from sitting on the bike, had collapsed beneath her. Heedless of her cries, I rode on, thinking only about seeing her later that evening. Phyllis was not amused but later saw the funny side.

Mr and Mrs Williams seemed to approve of me and we got on very well together. Mrs Williams had suffered poor health from an early age as a result of rheumatic fever and this had weakened her heart. She was a Rhondda girl, one of two sisters. Her name was Sarah Ellen Sheppard before marriage. Her sister was called May.

Although she was not in good health, Mrs Williams was a fantastic cook. She was also a talented musician having played at Bethania Chapel in Abertysswg.

Phyllis's father, Owen, was a miner. He was born in Anglesey. His father had been a captain at sea and when Owen was a child his father was lost during a storm off the treacherous Bay of Biscay. Owen's mother, a widow with five children, returned to her family in the Rhondda. Life had been tough for her and to support his family Owen went down the mine at the tender age of eleven. His elder brother was shell-shocked in the First World War and was unable to help. His other brother left home and became a bit of a rolling stone. Owen's mother and two sisters relied on the pittance of a wage Owen earned.

Phyllis found work as an assistant cook at the Methodist Chapel opposite their house. The Chapel also served as a school canteen. Phyllis did not go into service, as many girls did, because of her mother's health. At times, Mrs Williams lost the use of her legs for months on end, but she still managed to cook by sitting on a chair in front of the fire.

I enjoyed many a supper at their home. They were really good to me.

Six weeks after we met, Phyllis and I decided to get engaged. I was not in favour of a long engagement and I asked Phyllis to marry me six weeks later. She wanted to wait.

"It's now or never," I said.

So, Phyllis was an Easter bride. We were married at St David's Church, Fleur-de-lis. It was a beautiful little church with an avenue of tall trees lining the path leading to the entrance.

On the bright morning of our wedding, the song always associated with Judy Garland, and which we considered `our song', was played on the radio.

It was *Easter Parade*.

I stood at the altar in my best suit and spats. Phyllis wore a beautiful midnight blue gown with a sweetheart neck. Her eyes sparkled as a shaft of sunlight fell upon her lovely face. We made our vows, and to my relief the wedding service was short. It needed to be as we were the first in a line of forty couples getting married that morning.

As we left the church and walked towards the gates, the other thirty-nine couples waiting to get married shook our hands and wished us well.

We could not afford a photographer, but the memory is as vivid now as then.

We walked back to the house as man and wife. Mrs Williams did us proud. The meal was wonderful, better than a caterer could have managed. There was no honeymoon, but Phyllis, Edytha and her boyfriend Albert and I went to Cardiff. We all had a meal at the Continental Restaurant which was a special treat for us all.

Phyllis and I had no home of our own so we lived with her parents. We were able to share the rent and that helped them. It was something most couples had to do at the time.

There was no money for new furniture either. We were satisfied that we could purchase secondhand furniture and grateful to have it.

We dreamed of having a home of our own one day. Getting married at Easter meant there was the whole summer to get to know each other. Our trips at the weekends on the motorbike were our chance to be alone together.

The employment situation in the coal industry was reaching crisis point. By this time Aneurin Bevan was a rising star. He became the voice of the working class in South Wales. He was a man after my own heart and I admired his strength and determination to stand up for our rights.

Trade unionism was under threat and it was important for miners join the South Wales Miners' Federation. A union from the Midlands came to the Welsh valleys to try and undermine the South Wales Miners' Federation. The blacklegs of the 1926 General Strike were more than eager to join this Spencer Union, as we called it. But our union was determined to prevent the expansion of the Spencer Union into the valleys.

Several towns like Bedwas, Bedlinog and Trelewis were staunch company towns, loyal to the coal owners. Feeling between both factions ran high and eventually spilled over into violence. There was real anger towards the blackleg families and they were sent to Coventry.

Feelings were highest in the Rhondda Valley where unemployment had reached a critical point. Powell Duffryn, the main coal owners in the valley, were despised by every miner. If you did not go along with what Powell Duffryn wanted, your cards were waiting for you at pit top at the end of the shift. At Bedwas Colliery feelings were not particularity favourable towards members of the South Wales Miners' Federation.

I sensed things were going to turn nasty.

In late October, 1935, the miners at Nine Mile Point Colliery decided to stay down in order to oust those miners who were not members of the Federation. A secret meeting was arranged by Arthur Horner and Ness Edwards. It was held in Trethomas Workmen's Hall. They asked nine committee members, including myself, if we were prepared to stage a sit down strike at Bedwas the following morning. The intention was to smash the company union by our action.

The next morning the shift started normally until the moment came to take the necessary action to implement the strike. We stopped the journeys travelling into the coalface. This prevented the miners there from filling up the trams with coal. Many of the miners were members of the company union and were not keen to support the strike. I was instructed to visit another district underground to inform the miners there that there would be no trams coming from pit bottom to enable them to continue working.

On my way to that district I was confronted by the overman and the rider who operated the journeys. I explained the situation to the overman and whilst my back was turned the rider struck me on the back of the head with a spanner. Blood poured from my head. I staggered and fell between the journey rails, partly concussed. I was at the bottom of a slope, thirty yards from a stationery journey of trams. The two men made their back towards the journey, leaving me where I had fallen. As I recovered from the blow I crawled into a safety manhole at the side of the track. Suddenly, I heard the rumbling of the journey of trams moving along the rails and I realised that if I hadn't moved I would have been killed. Meanwhile, the overman and rider had disappeared into another district. I managed to struggle onto the coalface and told the miners the position regarding the sit down strike. Many were still reluctant to join us. I retraced my steps and made my way back to pit bottom to make my report. My comrades saw the blood on my face and head and asked me what had happened. Mr Austin Lane ordered me to go to the surface for treatment as stitches were necessary. I was reluctant to leave my colleagues, but he insisted.

The men were very angry and emotional when they heard what had happened to me and went in search of the overman and rider. They found the rider, but not the overman who had fled the scene towards the South Pit. The men proceeded to manhandle the rider, almost throttling him, but calmly and coolly Austin Lane brought them to their senses.

"Come on, lads, that's not the way," he said.

If the overman had been present, he too would have had rough treatment which he would have deserved.

Austin Lane remembered Arthur Horner's famous words, "Remember, a head of ice and a belly full of fire."

Thank goodness he diffused the situation, otherwise things could have gone badly for all of us. Meanwhile, the men at the coalface realised that there would be no work that day and returned to the pit bottom crossing our picket line, still refusing to support our stand against company unionism. I wanted to remain underground with my colleagues but was ordered to get first aid treatment. They remained underground for eight to nine days and their stand finally led to the complete destruction of the so-called Spencer Union. The South Wales Miners' Federation had won the battle and those reluctant miners finally joined our union.

On arrival at the treatment centre on pit top, Mr Arthur Horner and Mr Ness Edwards, who in later years was to become a Member of Parliament, were addressing a group of miners in the presence of a reporter from the South Wales Echo. Whilst I was receiving treatment they were informed of the incident and insisted that a photograph should be taken. Arthur Horner, Ness Edwards and myself, with my head heavily bandaged, posed in front of the camera. I made the headlines. Mr Ness Edwards kindly drove me home in his car and the family Doctor Arthur H Richards was summoned to stitch the wound. There were repercussions for myself and the others involved in the sit down strike at Bedwas Colliery. We were instantly dismissed, but our union ensured that our wages were paid until we found alternative employment.

We were unemployed for several months into the New Year. I eventually found work at Britannia Colliery which, luckily for me, was a Federation Colliery There was no compensation for my injury because I did not have sufficient means to take private action against the two men involved. A lot of water has flowed under the bridge since then. Both men have now passed on and I am not one to bear a grudge.

18 - *Death of a King, Birth of a Son*

Early in the New Year the whole nation was in mourning for King George V who died on 20th January, 1936. He was succeeded by his son Edward, Prince of Wales, who became Edward VIII. Here in South Wales Edward was loved and admired as a man of the people because he showed real interest and genuine concern for the unemployed workers during the Depression. He visited the Rhymney Valley to see the situation for himself and was dismayed to see the poverty and suffering in the valley, especially when visiting the town of Rhymney which had been titivated up by the local officials for the occasion. The cottages on the route to be taken had been white-washed, which covered a multitude of sins.

A man in the crowd shouted, "You have not seen the real poverty and squalor, your Royal Highness!"

Officials hustled the man away as quickly as they could but the Prince of Wales had heard his outburst and demanded to see everything. When he saw the reality of the situation he was appalled that people were living in such terrible conditions and said, "Something must be done."

We looked forward to his reign because we knew that in him we had a monarch who cared for his subjects.

It was doubly important for me to have employment at this time because Phyllis was expecting our first child in March. We were both looking forward to this great event in our lives and so were Owen and Sarah Ellen. Phyllis and I realised that it was time to find a home of our own but it was a question of waiting for the right place at the right price. We decided to remain with Phyllis's parents until the baby was born. Most births were at home in those days and were referred to as home confinements, with the mid-wife in attendance. On the first day of spring, 21st March, 1936, our son was born at 10 PM. I was very proud. A son. So important to a man to carry on the family name. Phyllis was adamant that the baby's first name should be John because this was a name that had been passed on from generation to generation in her family. His second name was a true Celtic name, Brian. Because there were several Johns in the family we decided to use this name. John Brian Morgan.

It is strange how a man becomes so possessive of his first born, especially a son, when it is his wife who has suffered to bring the child into this world.

Brian was the apple of everyone's eye, a healthy, bonny baby weighing ten and a half pounds - a real armful, with brown eyes. His hair, what little he had, was dark brown like his Mum's and Dad's. It's wonderful how a baby can bring such joy and Brian was certainly the centre of attraction. At weekends we would take him for walks in his second-hand pram which looked like new in the spring sunshine. It was a good thing that Phyllis was living with her mother during the early weeks because Sarah Ellen, although plagued by ill-health, was a fountain of knowledge for the over-anxious new mum. Our main concern was that Brian was disturbing Sarah Ellen's sleep during the night. Rest was important to her because of her heart problems.

We waited patiently until the right house came along and it turned out to be situated in the same street as my grandmother, number 13, Pwllglas Road, very near to Phyllis's parents. Sarah Ellen had a superstitious nature and worried about the street number. Phyllis was not at all concerned as her mother's superstitious nature had led her to reject what she thought of as old wives' tales.

Phyllis was delighted to be able to choose her own decor and implement her own ideas. Green was one of her favourite colours and the front parlour was decked out in green furnishings, carpet and curtains. Number 13 and the colour green. "Unlucky!" people cried. Phyllis did not worry one iota.

Within a few weeks, to a chorus of "I told you so!", I had an accident underground in Britannia Colliery. A large stone fell from the roof on top of me. I was in a kneeling position and my face was wedged against the ground while my back held the full weight of the stone. I gritted my teeth and used all my strength to hold the weight because if I collapsed I would have been crushed.

"Come and get this bloody stone off me," I shouted.

It took five men to lift that stone.

"I'm alright," I said, but was ordered home. How I managed to walk home from the colliery I do not know. For the next six weeks I was flat out on my back with every muscle in my body strained by my efforts to survive. A weaker man would have perished. Thank God I was still alive. Phyllis soon put those superstitious folk in their places and dismissed it by saying, "Don't talk daft. It would have happened wherever we were living, be it here or 24 Davies Street!"

Brian was thriving and was a good advert for Nestle's Baby Milk. He would have won any baby competition had he been entered. This was also considered unlucky by Phyllis's mother.

With a family now, I traded in my old bike for a BSA motorbike and sidecar in anticipation of summer weekends. Sarah Ellen was afraid that something dreadful would happen.

Cars were few and far between and mostly owned by doctors or the well-to-do members of society. We were a family and wanted to be together in all things we undertook but I now realised that my tearaway days were over. I had responsibilities and reduced my speed accordingly. There were no regrets. I had a great sense of belonging again. Now I had a real purpose to my life. My marriage and the birth of my son gave me complete satisfaction. This was my family.

While we were enjoying the British summer, events in Europe turned sour. Fascism was the word on everyone's lips here in South Wales and abroad. Until recently in Great Britain it had remained in the background but in the theatre of Europe it had taken centre-stage, especially in Germany and Italy. Fascism and the name of Adolf Hitler was spreading like wildfire across Europe and even began to penetrate the British Isles in the shape of Oswald Moseley. It was a threat to the trade unions and to the working classes. Fascism's arch enemy was communism which had found its footing here in South Wales during the miners' struggles of the thirties when the USSR had supported their cause. Its roots were laid down in the Rhondda Valley, with Arthur Horner, a leading Communist Party, member who had become the first Communist leader of the South Wales Miners' Federation in May. There were other communists within the Federation, like Will Paynter. With the outbreak of the Spanish Civil War on 16th July, 1936 there was a strong feeling amongst miners that the struggle in Spain between Loyalists, led by Franco, and Republicans was our struggle too. Under Franco, the Fascists were attempting to overthrow the democratically elected Republican Government. Our government decided not to interfere in this struggle, much to the dismay of several members of parliament, including Aneurin Bevan who believed fascism was a threat to democracy. However, the British government were to remain spectators in the Civil War. With the support of the USSR, the International Brigade was formed from the working classes and intellectuals in several countries. Men volunteered to fight for a cause they felt was just. Many of those brave men who fought for the Republican cause were miners from the valleys of South Wales, including Will Paynter. Some were never to return and lie on the Plains of Spain. Gone but not forgotten.

The other major event at that time was the conflict between King Edward VIII and the government, led by Baldwin, over the Mrs Simpson affair. It was obvious that the King was truly in love with Mrs Simpson. The British Constitution, the Monarchy and the Church did not recognise divorce or divorcees. It was a battle of wills and unfortunately the odds were stacked against this popular King. It must have been an unbearable situation for him and his abdication on 11th December, 1936 was a great shock. A king renouncing his throne for the woman he loved was an admirable decision on his part. The Duke of Windsor's (his new title) sacrifice brought greater love and respect from the ordinary people of his

Kingdom and he is remembered with great affection to this very day. By the time the nation got over the shock of his abdication he was already out of the country. Did the British government fear rebellion? With the present turmoil within the ranks of the royal family, things would probably have turned out differently for him. Fate decreed that there would be no children from his marriage to Mrs Simpson and our present Queen Elizabeth would still have become Queen eventually.

Brian's first Christmas. He was nine months old and we could not believe how time had flown. He was too young to really appreciate Christmas but our joy was complete. Christmas is a time for children. Looking at Brian, our thoughts turned to the baby born on Christmas Day, the Lord Jesus. Mary's joy was ours too.

Although Christmas was peaceful in Great Britain, the war in Spain raged on. It was getting bloodier by the minute and there were no shouts of Happy New Year. The main topic of conversation in 1937 was the impending Coronation of King George VI in May. Personally I was not interested in such matters because I hate pomp and ceremony. Others were looking forward to the Coronation with great eagerness. The first day of spring heralded Brian's first birthday. He was beginning to find his feet and was an early walker but a late talker. I longed for the day he would say Dada, just as much as Phyllis longed for him to say Mama.

The odds were with Phyllis at ten to one.

He was a bright, intelligent one year old and was getting heavy to carry around. He was a happy child and loved to hear Phyllis singing as she got on with her chores. Phyllis had a lovely voice and as a young girl she used to take part in the local operettas and plays in the village of Abertysswg where she had lived. Phyllis was a gregarious person, loved being with people and was liked by all her friends and neighbours. Her affectionate name among friends was `Smiler'. She always made the most dreary day light up for those who met her.

Brian was going to be like his Mum, of that I was certain.

I was a more serious type and did not make friends easily. Opposites attract, so they say. Phyllis was a good wife and whatever shift I worked, be it days, afternoons or nights, she was always there to see me off to work. With my grandmother living close by, Phyllis used to spend a pleasant hour or two chatting and it was from my grandmother that Phyllis learned all about my difficult childhood. With this knowledge, Phyllis was determined to make my life as happy as possible. Although her own upbringing had been tough and regimented, it had been happier than mine and she did her utmost to try and create the happiness I had lost.

Our second wedding anniversary arrived and like most men, I forgot. I was in the dog-house for a few days. Women are such sentimental creatures about things like that. My mind was on earning a living for my family, much more important in my eyes. My birthday came and went. I was just another year older as far as I was concerned. I have never really been interested in things like that but now I realise how important they are to a woman.

During the latter part of April there were frenzied activities going on in the community in preparation for the Coronation of George VI and Queen Elizabeth on 12th May, 1937. Street parties were being planned for the children. Everyone hoped it would not rain. There were committees for this and committees for that. The petty squabbles between the ladies were highly amusing to Phyllis. Everybody wanted to do a celebration cake but somebody had to do the sandwiches, little cakes and trifles.

In the days leading up to the Coronation, women were frantically cooking and baking and men were practically banished from the kitchens. In Sarah Ellen's larder there were cakes of every kind: fruit cakes, plain cakes, tea cakes, apple tarts, welsh cakes and my favourite, iced slices. It was surprising what was achieved with a couple of pounds of flour, fruit and all the other ingredients thrown in. The men's task on the day was to carry the parlour tables from the houses and line them along the street. The best table cloths were spread and dishes laid out in regimental order. Everyone was ushered to their allotted seat and the feast was well and truly under-way. For one day at least the daily struggles of life were set aside and everyone really enjoyed themselves. The children enjoyed it most of all. Coronation medals were minted to commemorate events, as with every Coronation, and would be treasured mementoes for many years to come. The womenfolk did us proud and everyone had a good time.

Tomorrow was another day.

Brian was getting used to the sound of the motorbike and we used to get away some weekends to the countryside. There was one particular incident in Herefordshire that would definitely have made a scene in a *Carry On* film. It was not funny at the time but was hilarious afterwards. We were travelling along a narrow country lane in the motorbike and sidecar. Brian was asleep in Phyllis's arms when, to our horror, we saw a massive bull racing towards us with farm-hands chasing him. He must have weighed at least a ton. Phyllis began to panic and cried out, "Reg! Reg! Do something quickly."

The lane seemed too narrow to turn the motorbike around but that is exactly what I attempted to do. I did a wheely with the sidecar almost vertical on the bank. How Phyllis and Brian were not thrown out I do not know. I raced hell for leather and with the bull snorting close behind us we shot past an open gate. Luckily for us, the bull ran through the gate and into the open field. Finally, it was brought under control by the farmer and farm hands. I pulled into a lay-by to recover from this close encounter and then decided to walk back along the lane to see the bull for myself. Phyllis stayed put. She wanted nothing to do with it. When I saw the size of the bull I agreed with her.

During this summer, Sarah Ellen's health had deteriorated slightly and Phyllis, being an only child, thought it was her duty to care for her mother but felt torn as we loved being in our own home. Phyllis was worried how I would react to the possibility of giving up our home to go and live with her parents. But she need not have worried. Sarah Ellen had been good to me and after we had discussed the situation we made our decision to move back to live with her parents. We felt it was the right decision.

We soon got into the old routine of sharing a house again and at weekends when Owen was able to take care of Sarah Ellen we could get out and about again.

We certainly made the most of the summer months. On one particular weekend I decided to take Brian and Phyllis to my favourite spot, the Royal Forest of Dean. We were travelling towards Usk at a place called Glascoed, passing a public house called the Horse and Jockey. A red and white bus pulled into the side to pick up some passengers. The road was clear ahead and the driver waved me onwards. As I began to overtake the bus, a car shot out from the public house, blocking my path. I had to make a lightning decision to prevent a collision with the car and the only way clear was the lane from which the car had come. I turned into the lane very sharply and the motorbike and sidecar tipped over. I landed upside down by a gate on the grass and Phyllis, who was cradling Brian's head, was thrown out onto a gravel path.

The bus driver and several passengers ran to our aid, together with a middle-aged couple who were travelling in the car behind us. Brian was swiftly taken from Phyllis's arms and the lady from the car cradled Phyllis's head in her lap. By now I had come round and rushed to where Phyllis was lying. Her face was covered in blood and badly torn by the gravel. The shock of seeing her like that made me pass out cold. Everyone thought that Phyllis was unconscious, but she later told me that she was aware of everything.

People were saying, "Poor girl, her face is ruined for life. Get some brandy for her."

The landlord of the public house said that there was a doctor's house close by and the middle-aged couple offered to take the three of us in their car. Unfortunately, this doctor was recovering from nervous strain and said that he just could not tackle such a delicate injury.

"You'll have to take her to hospital," he said.

"No. I want to go home and Doctor Richards will attend to me," said Phyllis.

The couple who had come to our aid kindly took us home, right to our front door.

Sarah Ellen was taking her usual Sunday nap after dinner and upon waking, she saw Phyllis being brought into the house with her face in bandages and also Brian and myself with bandages swathed around our heads. It was a great shock for her, but for the moment her own health was put aside and her main concern was for Phyllis, whose injuries were far worse than ours. Doctor Richards was called out and his response was immediate. He proceeded to clean Phyllis's face and decided that she needed stitches. Thirty-six stitches were required and Doctor Richards had to do this without anaesthetic. Phyllis did not even whimper. She clenched her fists and gritted her teeth. Her threshold to withstand pain was unbelievable. She was truly a very brave young woman. Her faith in Doctor Richards never left her.

After treating Phyllis, Doctor Richards applied two stitches to Brian's wounds and proceeded to check my reflexes, because of the bump on my head. He told us that Phyllis was a lucky girl because the impact of her accident had only been a third of an inch from the temple. His anxiety was about the possible disfigurement to Phyllis's face. Ten days later the bandages were removed, not by Doctor Richards but by his young colleague. Doctor Richards was looking through the window with his back to Phyllis. He was afraid to look at her for a few seconds.

The other doctor said, "It's alright, Doctor. You can turn around now."

He turned around slowly. His smile told the whole story. Through his skill, Phyllis's face had healed beautifully, with only a faint scar at the temple and one above the upper lip. Her beautiful face, thank God, had not been ruined for life. It was a day for celebration and grateful thanks to that wonderful doctor.

It was now time to trace the culprit who had caused the accident. The middle-aged couple had managed to take his number as he fled the scene of the crime. Court action was taken and the driver admitted he was under the influence of drink. The court awarded Phyllis seventy pounds compensation, which was a lot of money in those days.

Phyllis never rode on a motorbike again. She had completely lost her confidence which, under the circumstances was a normal reaction. However, I decided to have another motorbike because it was convenient for getting to work. It was the Velocette, a very fast and powerful bike. Phyllis hated the sight of it so I kept it in the garage where she could not see it.

Sarah Ellen suffered a further stroke a few months later. Doctor Richards said it was delayed reaction from the shock she had when she saw us being brought into the house on the day of the accident. The stroke left her partially paralysed down one side and Phyllis had the added responsibility of nursing her mother. It was a great strain on her, but she coped very well. We both felt a sense of responsibility for her condition and Phyllis wished sometimes that she had gone to hospital and not insisted on coming home on the day of the accident. But at times like that you do not think of the consequences.

19 - *Outbreak of War*

Our problems were nothing compared to the suffering of the people in Spain. There was anger in the hearts of the decent folk in the valleys and in my soul at the atrocities taking place in Spanish towns and villages. I felt a strong urge to join the International Brigade but I suppressed it because I had a young wife and child and felt my responsibilities rested with them.

I was now working at Pengam Housecoal Colliery with Owen who was overman there, responsible for planning the work underground. To be an overman was a step up the social ladder in the community's eyes and some of the miners would offer bribes, in kind not cash, to gain favours. But Owen would have none of it.

Once again my team mates were the pit horses who lived most of their lives underground, apart from the miners' fortnight's holiday each July. These were big strong horses and needed to be to pull the loaded trams to pit bottom. Most hostlers were kind and considerate to their dumb friends and would bring a tit-bit or two for them. Some, however, were not and I, being a straightforward chap, told them exactly what I thought of them.

Kindness always brought greater rewards than cruelty.

Pengam was the `Wellington Mine' and you certainly needed them. The water underground flowed like a river and it was difficult to walk against the flow. In my view, Pengam Colliery was the wettest pit in Wales. It was not a really deep mine, only about six hundred feet from the surface, but the water gushed in torrents through the roof. Electrical pumps were in operation twenty four hours a day. Otherwise we would have needed aqualungs and the horses would have drowned. There were two big pumps, four smaller pumps and thirty blast pumps which kept everything under control. There were no pithead baths and you worked all the shift in wet clothes and went home wet. Mining is a tough job and to really understand it you have to work in a mine. You earned every penny in sweat and toil, but the miners still did not get a fair and decent wage for their efforts.

Would we ever get a fair deal?

The colliery was nearer home, although uphill most of the way. After a long day's hard work, it was like climbing Mount Everest. When I arrived home,

Phyllis had already positioned the tin bath in front of the fire and had the hot water close at hand. It was wonderful to wash off the dirt and grime of the colliery, put on dry clean clothes and settle down to a good hot dinner. A miner's wife was the salt of the earth.

Phyllis's twenty-fifth birthday was on 5th July and we celebrated quietly at home with the family. I would have liked to have taken her out for a fish and chip supper but we could not leave Brian with Sarah Ellen because of her fragile health. Phyllis was very understanding and was happy enough with a few cards and small gifts, like a scarf or brooch. We could still have our fish and chip supper at home.

I had changed my motorbike yet again. Uncle Jack, who lived in Fochriw, now had the fast and powerful Velocette, which took some handling. I deeply regretted selling Uncle Jack that bike. His body was found on a mountain road. He had failed to negotiate a bend and was killed outright. God rest his soul. His death still haunts me to this day.

For the next few months his accident lay heavily on my soul as I struggled with my conscience. In this frame of mind I decided to volunteer for the International Brigade but when I arrived at the South Wales Miners' Federation offices, Will Paynter said that there was no point in going out to Spain. Between July and November, the Loyalist Republicans had been routed by the Fascists and the International Brigade was being disbanded. The miners who had fought in the campaign and survived returned to Wales dejected and disillusioned. Fascism under Franco was winning the war and this was the beginning of the end for the Loyalists.

We prepared to celebrate Christmas far away from the troubles in Spain.

Sarah Ellen was famous for her Christmas cake recipe and it was a closely guarded secret apart from our immediate family. Although she was unable to prepare the cake herself, Phyllis followed her instructions. The mix was placed in prepared loaf tins and taken to the bakery in the village as our kitchen oven was too small for two large tins. The baker did his best to get the recipe from Phyllis but she would not reveal the secret.

It was wonderful to see the delight on Brian's face as we opened his Christmas presents: a little wooden train and the bane of every parent's life, a toy drum. We had a scrumptious Christmas dinner, including one of Owen's chickens.

Phyllis and I could not believe that Brian was approaching his third birthday. It seemed only yesterday that he was a babe in arms. He was a real roly-poly, but a happy, inquisitive child.

On April Fool's Day the Civil War in Spain came to its bitter end. One by one European countries were being incorporated into the German Reich and it was fast becoming evident that Hitler's ambition was to dominate both Western and Eastern Europe.

Our local grocer was convinced that war with Germany was inevitable and would be declared before the end of the year. He advised Phyllis to stock up on essential goods like sugar and flour. Sarah Ellen and Phyllis took heed of his warning and began to fill the larder week by week.

Hitler, however, was determined to dominate the world and when he invaded Poland on 1st September, 1939. War was declared on Germany two days later.

Britain was ill-prepared for this war, unlike Germany who had been preparing for war for several years.

Poland fell very quickly and other countries would follow. Working in the coal mines was considered a reserved occupation and I could have sat out the war in the mines. But once again my loyalties were divided between my family and my conscience. For several months I struggled with my conscience until I finally reached a decision. I was going to enlist in the army. My wife and child were in danger from this mad man.

I was twenty eight and full of fire.

20 - *Off to War*

There was Taffy, the Welsh miner, a good lad with his mitts,
And the Cockney bloke from Hoxton, wot kept us all in fits
An' Ginger in the Cook-house, and Nobby in the Store,
An' Scottie the Footballer, and a couple of hundred more.[1]

In December, 1939 I volunteered for the Armed Forces. I enlisted at Newport in Monmouthshire, now Gwent. Although I was accepted, if the true facts were known the Army could have sent me back to the coal mines. I altered my occupation on my marriage certificate from collier to surface labourer. Phyllis and her father thought I was mad. A lot of men preferred to enter a reserved occupation to avoid call up, which is only human suppose. Important jobs, the government would say. Lack of guts and courage I would call it. Politicians start wars, but you and me have to go out and fight them. We were expendable, yet I felt it was my duty to enlist.

I joined the Pioneer Corps, the pick and shovel mob. Three weeks of back breaking work constructing defences along the coast at Clacton-on-Sea. The mob consisted of first timers like myself and old timers from the First World War. I became particularly friendly with one old timer, a Welshman who told me how he had received a bayonet wound in the hip and showed me the scar. One night a young fellow who had been out drinking picked on the old timer. I was having none of that. When he turned on me I hit him three times and he slid down the door. It took several men to hold me back. He was out for the count anyway.

In the cold light of day he came up to me and apologised. He shook my hand.

"What a fool I was," he said.

"A drunken man will never get the better of a man who is sober," I replied.

After Clacton-on-Sea, our next stop was Skegness for further military

---

[1] Lt-Col H C Wheatley, OBED late CO 45 Group Royal Pioneers. *The Pioneer*, No II, Vol 2, June 1947

training, then to Leeds where we were guarding deserters and finally guard duty at York barracks. Following that we were sent to Southampton where we boarded a ship for Le Havre.

For the next few days we did more military training and then we were transported by cattle truck, forty men per truck, to Epernay, east of Paris. There we unloaded ammunition which was sent to the front line.

A few weeks later the Germans broke through our line of defence, the Maginot Line. Our camp at Epernay was bombed and we retreated. The roads were crowded with thousands of refugees fleeing their homes. One family were sitting on the side of the road crying. They were trying to get to Bordeaux and their vehicle had run out of petrol. My friend and I took pity on them. We managed to rustle up a few gallons which helped them on their way.

We were heading for Northwest France. The Germans were pushing forward to capture the Channel ports. We continued our retreat via the beautiful Loire Valley, through Orleans, Tours, Angers and Nantes. We helped to construct an airfield and destroyed equipment left by retreating troops. At five o' clock one morning we were told to muster in the local square.

"Well boys, I am awfully sad to tell you that the Germans have captured most of the Channel ports. From here on it's every man for himself," our Major said.

There might be a chance if we could get to St Nazaire, he thought. It was either that or a dash to the South of France then across the border into Spain.

Our chances were not good.

Some First World War veterans said they were not going to run away from the Germans. The veterans disappeared into the woods never to be seen again. Others made their way towards Spain. Whether they got there or not, I never found out.

The majority decided on St Nazaire. We arrived at midday and waited for embarkation. A Cunard liner called the Lancastria was at anchor in the bay. I heard she had six thousand troops on board and was ready to sail. We waited on the dock. A destroyer, the Highlander docked. Some men boarded her whilst I went with my pals to board the Oronsay. Two German bombers flew over. We thought the Highlander was the target, but the Oronsay was hit. Even so we continued to board her. Rope ladders were thrown over the side for us to climb onto her deck. Once we were settled on deck the bombers returned and attacked the Lancastria, still at anchor in the bay. Three bombs were released across the ship and within twenty minutes the ship slipped between the waves with thousands of troops clinging to her side as she went under. Some were swimming in the sea around her and the German planes kept up their attack by machine gunning the struggling troops in the water.

I was an eyewitness to the whole tragedy on 17th June, 1940 at 3.45 PM Other ships in the vicinity rescued those who survived the sea attack.

It was estimated at the time that we lost three thousand three hundred troops on the Lancastria. We were so exhausted that we picked the warmest spot on the Oronsay, the engine room, and settled down to sleep. The next thing we knew we had arrived in Plymouth Harbour. We were lucky to get back because we had still been in France nine days after the evacuation of Dunkirk. Unknown to me, Phyllis had received all my letters from the War Office with the following statement: "Believed Missing in Action."

We arrived at Plymouth on 18th June to a hero's welcome. The band played us into the quay. We were exhausted yet we marched proudly to the railway station to board the train that would take us to London. We stopped at Exeter and were treated like lords with tea, cakes and lots of goodies. When we arrived in London, we spent our first night sleeping in the Albert Hall. Floors, seats, balconies, you name it. Anywhere we could bed down in reasonable comfort.

I could not remember the last time I had slept in a real bed and I longed to be home.

Our billet was a school in Hackney Wick. Temporary, because it fell victim to German bombs in 1940. As I was still in the Pioneer Corps. It was our Company's job to clear debris after bombing raids.

Whilst involved with this work my Company required volunteers for a vehicle repair and maintenance course at Walthamstow Technical College. Being mechanically minded I applied for the course. Whilst attending, and carrying out bombing raid clearance duties, my friend and I inadvertently stepped over the white embarkation line of a bombed out building. We were arrested by a detective and taken to Wormwood Scrubs. From prison, I wrote to Phyllis. The name of the prison was on the envelope and Phyllis was unable to bring herself to open it, saying, "Reg has killed somebody. He is in gaol. It's that terrible temper of his."

There was panic until her father opened the letter and then relief at the contents. No one at the prison thought to inform the Company Commander of our whereabouts and the College authorities at Walthamstow reported us as deserters. When it came to light in court, our Major hit the roof. The dressing down which he would normally give to his own troops, he meted out to the detective. It made the detective look about six inches tall.

We were released immediately and returned to our course at Walthamstow. I passed my exams and was transferred to Bournemouth Technical College for a further course which lasted a month. After qualifying, I went to Aberfield for a course on tanks, bren gun carriers and lorries, mainly connected with recovery in the field of fire. This lasted for a month or two. When the course was completed, our group was transferred to the 56th London Division. We joined the 168 Infantry Brigade which was made up of the London Irish, London Scottish and Royal Berkshire Regiments. Our training took place in East Anglia at Coggeshall, Sudbury and Bury St Edmunds in the dead of winter, 1941. We were billeted in tents which offered no protection from the bitterly cold north east winds. No mountains here to protect us from the icy blast. We were in vests and short pants doing keep fit exercises in a vain attempt to keep warm. You had to be tough to survive.

I did not mind guard duty by day but really hated it at night as I am unable to sleep during the day.

When the sergeant said, "Anyone want to get off guard duty?" I jumped at the chance.

"I've got just the job for you," he said.

What a fool I was. I spent all day from dawn to dusk peeling potatoes. I had learned my lesson. Never volunteer.

An advantage of being stationed in Britain was regular home leave. It was a long way to travel but a great joy to see Phyllis and Brian, Owen and Sarah Ellen. A few precious hours was better than nothing at all. Phyllis was now expecting our second child and we both wanted a girl. Then we would have the pigeon pair. We looked forward to the birth and I wondered if I would be there to see our baby before going back overseas.

The months passed swiftly. Christmas, 1941 was to be the last Christmas I would spend with my family until the end of the war. In another two months our baby would arrive. Please God let me be here to see my baby.

Training was becoming intensive and we knew that something was going to erupt sooner or later. My prayers were answered. The baby was due any day now and I was given special leave to go home. It was late February and a typical winter's day. Our second child was in no hurry to be born and Phyllis was in labour more than twelve hours. She was having a rough time and the midwife was impatient to get home. So much so that she began to force the birth and at one stage Phyllis was on her knees. I thought to myself, If this is what having a child is like, there will be no more.

At six in the morning of 24th February our baby daughter was born. Her guessed weight was twelve and a half pounds. Within two hours of her birth our baby suffered a haemorrhage. Owen nursed the baby while the doctor was sent for. On the doctor's arrival, the comment from the midwife was, "She's a dying baby."

Doctor Richards turned to her and said, "Dying baby be buggered. Look at her lovely pink cheeks. This is the last baby that you will deliver."

The doctor tried to give the baby blood transfusions in the house but the needle kept clogging and we decided there was no alternative but to send Phyllis and the baby to Cardiff Royal Infirmary. Phyllis gave the baby the first blood transfusion and was then sent home by ambulance. The sister on the John Nixon Ward gave her the second transfusion. I was told that the baby was not expected to live. When I got home, Phyllis in desperation blamed me and refused to speak to me for several days until Owen brought her to her senses.

"This boy has to go back to the war. If the baby has to die it's better now, before you get to know her," he said.

"But Dad, it's her eyes. They haunt me," Phyllis replied.

It was a traumatic week for all of us. The baby seemed a little better after the transfusions but had lost a lot of her weight. By the end of the week there were shouts of, "It's a miracle."

There she was, my daughter Elaine, kicking her tiny legs in the air in her cot. Thank you God, thank you, I thought. Soon Elaine (named after Pearl White's series, *The Adventures of Elaine*, was brought home and the last vision of her, which was to remain with me throughout the war, was of her lying on two cushions smiling in her funny way. I returned to East Anglia and we were told that we were now returning to active duty. From Bury St. Edmunds we travelled by train to Greenock in Scotland, disembarked and marched in regular formation to the last known Liberty boat[2] waiting in the harbour, to set sail in convoy.

Destination unknown.

---

2 American name for a troop carrying ship.

21 - *To the Bay of Biscay and Beyond*

We sailed on the evening tide, a convoy of destroyers, cruisers and Liberty boats, hoping to avoid contact with the German U-boats. For the next six weeks, the sea was our constant companion. Our boat was the California and our duties were in the Crows Nest, manning the Halican gun in case of aerial attack. Whether we would have managed to hit the planes is open to doubt because of mountainous seas. We were not sailors and so you can imagine how we felt. One minute we were touching the heavens, the next minute we were in hell.

Oh for the sight of land.

From the Irish Sea to the Bay of Biscay, way out into the Atlantic Ocean. At last we sighted terra firma: Sierra Leone, the port of Freetown. We were at anchor in the bay for several days but were not allowed ashore. Training on deck was our rest. Local people offered fruit from their boats which we purchased eagerly, lowering money in tins from the deck to their boats. The fruit was then hauled aboard.

We set sail from Freetown out into the Atlantic. Attempting to avoid U-boats, we headed for the coast of South America, towards Rio de Janeiro then back again to the Cape of Good Hope and on to Capetown. What a beautiful vista. The city with Table Mountain as its background rose from sea level to the lap of the gods. After weeks at sea it was heaven. We came into harbour to the strain of bagpipes played by the London Scottish Regiment. This visit was to be the best ten days of my life as I enjoyed the sunshine, sea and sparkling white sandy beaches. We were billeted in tents at the foot of Table Mountain and I would have remained there but for the kindness of Mr and Mrs Grace who owned a small vineyard.

An English couple, the Graces were originally from Essex but had been in South Africa for many years. They took me and my pal, Tommy Thomas from Walsall, all around Cape Province and invited us to their beautiful bungalow. We also ventured out on our own but were warned not to mix with `the coloureds'. One evening we visited a cinema. When the lights went up during the interval we realised we were the only white men there. People smiled at us and we felt like honoured guests. An old man invited us to his shanty home and we saw at first hand the conditions black people were living in. We were appalled. We did not agree with the apartheid system.

The next day we were due to depart on a new Dutch liner called the New Amsterdam. The liner was undefended - no escort this time. We sailed past Madagascar into the Indian Ocean making our way to Alexandria in Egypt through the Red Sea. We disembarked at a port at the lower end of the Suez Canal and boarded a train for Alexandria. On arrival we pitched tents on the outskirts of Alexandria. We found a wooden hut in which to doss down. After quarter of an hour we began to itch all over. Our mosquito nets gave no relief or protection. The truth finally dawned: the hut was bug infested and we had no sleep that night of the battle of the bugs. We would rather sleep in the desert with the scorpions for companions.

Life in Egypt seemed almost biblical. One day we saw a man riding a donkey, with his eight wives trailing behind, carrying bundles of wood and other goods on their heads. Two wives began to quarrel. The husband dismounted the donkey and started to thrash the women with a stick. Us lads, protested but he took no notice and went on his way.

The canal served every purpose: clothes washing, ablutions, lavatory and repository for animal carcasses. Water was also drawn for drinking purposes by the women of the villages. They transported it by carrying jars on their heads.

Although we were at war, there was the opportunity for leave to explore Alexandria and Cairo. This gave us chance to purchase a few souvenirs. There were carpets, leather work, metal work, filigree and jewelled daggers. We were always on the alert to possible danger, with one chap guarding our rear. In Cairo, the shoe shine boys were everywhere. Woe betide you if you did not have your shoes cleaned. They would pour the shoe polish over your legs and shorts. A good kick up the backside was our answer to such treatment. On one of our sorties in Cairo, Tommy Thomas and I went into a restaurant for a quiet drink, or so we thought. In came some Australians from front line duty. They took over the restaurant. Tables were lined up, crates of beer were stacked on top and the Australians began to drink. After a while some, the worse for drink, slipped under the table. Then the trouble started. Chairs and bottles began to fly. We made a swift exit before the Red Caps eventually turned up. Fists were flying and the Australians ended up in clink, to be bailed out later by their officer. They were hard drinking and hard headed but damn good fighters, being both reliable and steadfast in battle.

Leave over, military training continued at Alexandria in preparation for impending action. Information had been gathered showing evidence that the Germans were pushing towards Egypt. Our task was to hold the line at El Alamein. There was a temporary lull in the fighting because the Germans were unable to gather their equipment together for a sustained battle. It was decided that our Division be withdrawn from the desert for other duties. The reason for our departure was due to the fact that the Germans were pushing down through the Caucasus Mountains. We travelled via the Sinai Desert into Palestine and from there to Jordan and over the mountain range into Iraq, making camp in Baghdad near the Royal Palace.

During the first few nights we lost several rifles and a machine gun. The culprits were working their way into camp under cover of darkness. Lights were placed around the camp perimeter and we were ordered to shoot on sight. Chains were issued, with the order to lock rifles around the wrist. Rifles were also buried under the sand and the order was to sleep on them. There were several incidents and as instructed we opened fire. The next day there was a warning from the palace: if we did not refrain from shooting towards the palace, royal guards would return fire. Message received and understood!

It was in Baghdad that we encountered our first refugees, mostly women and children whom we believed to be Jews making their way towards Palestine from Eastern bloc countries.

A few weeks later our Division, 56th London, was ordered to proceed north to the Iraqi Persian border. We were to defend this area in case the Germans broke through the mountains to capture the oil wells at Kirkuk. We spent part of the very wet, cold winter in this area. We slept in tents, withstanding mud, wind, rain, ice and heavy snowfalls. We had to take turns holding the tent pole in case it blew away in the wind.

Our diet was bully beef and biscuits. The beef was cut into pieces and served as stew and the biscuits were mashed. Occasionally we managed to purchase an egg or two from the Kurds. All our allies had better grub than we did, especially the Aussies, Americans and New Zealanders. They say an army marches on its stomach. It was a miracle we could march at all.

The Kurds seemed a strange people to Western eyes. They built their villages on top of a mound and surrounded them with mud walls. There was no proper entrance such as a door or gateway, just windows cut in the walls which served as look-outs and entries. We supposed this was for defensive purposes. We met a Kurdish man and asked how he would go about killing an enemy. His reply was, "Two fingers in the eyes, catch hold of the hair, pull the head down and knife up and under into the heart." Enough said.

One day we heard sounds like the local jazz bands back home. Our curiosity got the better of us and we went to investigate. It was a funeral procession and a very serious matter to the Kurds. The men gave us menacing looks and we decided that retreat was the best course of action.

Kirkuk had to be safeguarded at all costs because of the oil which was piped as far as Haifa in Israel. Fresh orders were received. Once again our division was on course for a speedy return to Egypt. We retraced our steps the way we came and arrived back in Alexandria. The reason for this manoeuvre was the now famous Battle of El Alamein. In preparation for the impending battle we practised military manoeuvres in the desert to acclimatise ourselves for desert warfare. Sand, shit and flies. Nine whole months of it. No time for spit and polish, just fighting and trying to survive the best way we could. We lived, ate and slept sand.

The second battle of El Alamein was about to commence. The battle for Egypt.

At 2130 hours on 23rd October we opened up with everything in our possession: anti-tank guns, long toms, twenty five pounders and Bofors guns. On this offensive we managed to break through the German lines. Our comrades in arms consisted of the 9th Australian Division, 51st Highland Division, New Zealand Division, First South African Division, 4th Indian Division, 50th Division (my group), 44th Division, 7th Armoured Division and one French brigade. We broke through the German lines at a place called Tell el Aqqaqir. The New Zealanders were the first group to break through and from that point onwards the Germans and Italians were on the run.

We pushed them all the way back to Tobruk.

Upon arrival at Tobruk, our brigade, the 50th Division, was withdrawn to Alexandria in Egypt to combine with two other brigades connected with the London 56th Division. Our divisional sign was the black cat, unlucky for some but lucky for me. Something was afoot.

On the outskirts of Alexandria our military training involved practise and preparations for sea landings. Invasion was imminent. But where?

We were soon to find out.

At Alexandria we boarded a ship and set sail for the invasion of Sicily. The sea was very rough and certainly made the lads seasick. We were not in any condition to make a landing. On 10th July, 1943, the 8th Army landed at Syracuse in Sicily.

22 - *Invasion of Sicily*

The landing at Syracuse was a very sad time.

"You stick to me and you'll be okay," I used to say to my pal Taffy from North Wales.

But at Syracuse we were separated. He was in the transport group and I was with the landing party. Whilst my pal was still on board ship it was attacked by Stuka dive bombers. The ship took several direct hits and exploded.

God rest his soul and all those who were on board.

One special memento of Syracuse which I carried throughout the war was a rosary. I still have it to this day. I am sure it brought me home safely from the war.

I wish it could have saved my pal.

Syracuse eventually fell and we foot slogged north to Augusta. The Sicilians had fled to the hills and left their farms and live-stock unattended.

Augusta finally taken, we pushed onwards to a ridge close to Catania. My duty there was to man a machine gun post on a bend in the road. There was a lot of troop movement on that particular road. One day about noon, two Italian planes came in low above the road which was full of troops. The first plane was in the sights of my gun. As it came in I opened fire. There was an explosion in the fuel tank and thick black smoke belched from the plane. It crashed into the valley. The second plane fled towards Catania.

Some of our troops were killed and others badly wounded. As they lay on the ground, men cried out for their mothers.

Then there was a lull, apart from German shell fire along the ridge. Our troops advanced during the night and the Germans lit up the sky with flares and mortars.

The next morning Tommy Thomas and I went down to the valley to look at the burnt out remains of the plane I had hit. The pilot was still in the cockpit, his body charred. My immediate feeling was pity that this had to happen. Later that feeling faded as we came across a German pill-box and saw several of our men lying dead around it. They had captured it, but at a cost.

The 168th London Division comprising the London Scottish, Irish and Royal Berkshire Regiment were trying to advance along the plain at Catania. Resistance was heavy but we finally pushed the Germans back. As we moved forward we were under constant fire from their rear guard.

It was sunny weather at the time but the view was anything but pleasant. Dead German bodies were lying where they had fallen, plus several bloated carcasses of horses. The stench was sickening. We referred to this place as `Stinky Horse Corner'. There was one corpse lying near to where I stood. He had ginger hair and as I turned him over I let him drop back quickly. His face was crawling with maggots. He was a corporal and at least six feet tall. A German scout car which was on the road had taken a direct shell hit. The driver's legs were broken and his shin bones were sticking out. The officer's body was still in the seat, minus his head. On his helmet was his name, Lt. DeWinter. He was a powerfully built man with broad shoulders. He must have been fine looking.

What a waste of life.

Constantly under fire from artillery and machine guns and with the added danger of land mines, we proceeded to Catania Bridge with the aim of capturing a large building. It was full of huge wine vats.

The following morning some of the lads were reprimanded for being drunk on duty.

At dawn I heard a sound under the floor and I discovered a nanny goat trapped in the basement. I released her and watched as she climbed up into the mountains. All around there were vineyards full of grapes. Some of the vines were booby trapped and we lost three men.

Warrant Officer Scrivens from Macclesfield said the old man (the Captain) wanted me to salvage equipment from a wireless truck that had been knocked out of action in no man's land.

My first reaction was to retort, "You've got fellows with stripes to do the job, sir. I've got a wife and kids at home."

He replied, "Ah but Taff, the old man has chosen you."

The Captain and I drove off in the jeep to no man's land. He instructed me to remain there until he returned from seeing an officer about something. Hours rolled by. As dawn broke, a London Irish officer approached me and said, "What the hell are you doing here? We're going to open up with everything we can throw at the Germans in a minute!"

I told him I was waiting for the Captain to return but I did not need to be told twice when he ordered me out. The Captain was recalled. An educated man who could speak seven languages, he was useless as a front line officer.

During the night a German soldier burst into the barn where we were billeted. He gave us a fright. But the poor bugger had had enough and he raised his hands and surrendered.

We failed to catch up with the bulk of the retreating German army so we pushed on to Messina. This was officially the end of the Sicilian Campaign. Local people were trying to gather in the harvest so we helped them. It was a good thing for us to do after the carnage we had seen.

We withdrew back to Catania and remained there for a few weeks, relaxing. When he learned I was the proud owner of a hair cutting kit, the commanding officer, who had a beautiful head of curly hair, ordered me to cut it all off. I was nervous but gave him a short back and sides. I was then ordered to cut the whole Company's hair and from dawn to dusk that is exactly what I did. The boys were appreciative and gave me money and cigarettes.

I was suffering recurring bouts of malaria but kept quiet because I did not want to be separated from my group. I would have ended up in a transit camp whilst the others moved on and I would never have caught up.

General Montgomery paid us a visit and informed us that the next offensive would be Italy. Monty was well liked by the troops because we felt he was straight with us. He told Churchill exactly what was needed and would not budge until he got what he wanted.

Monty was undoubtedly one of the finest Generals of the War.

Our first encounter with the Americans was in Palermo, Sicily. A local girl had been molested by a soldier. My pal and I were walking through the town when an American came up to us waving his revolver around and asking who we were. I told him to point his gun elsewhere. The culprit turned out to be one of his own crowd. They were very fond of young girls. The Americans flashed money, chocolates and silk stockings around.

The lads used to call them cradle snatchers.

23 - *Crossing the Straits*

It was dusk when we arrived in Palermo and were ordered to embark on landing crafts. The weather was set against us. We had a rough crossing through the Messina Straits and seasickness was rife. Our destination was Salerno and the Germans knew we were coming. The next morning under heavy fire, we fixed bayonets as the landing craft ramp was lowered. Wading into the sea, water to our waists, we discovered that the Germans had laid barbed wire. A lot of men did not make it to the beach. Those of us who did headed for the nearest cover. Fighting continued all day. We managed to advance inland, capturing the village of Sarno by nightfall.

After a short rest in Sarno we commenced our forward push towards Naples. Fighting continued all the way though resistance was light. The Germans were retreating from Naples.

To boost our moral, the brass put on a special show for us in Naples which we enjoyed as best we could under the circumstances. The following day we moved out towards Capua. One night I was on guard duty. Nearby, a Gurkha Company guarded their own lines. It was pitch black and unknown to me a Gurkha inadvertently wandered into our lines. I had a strange sensation at the back of my neck and my hair stood on end.

"It's all right, Tommy," he said.

I froze and slowly turned around. I could just make out his white teeth glistening. I was happy he was on our side. I am sure I would have been decapitated if he had been the enemy.

Malaria finally betrayed me to the medical officer. He gave me a terrible dressing down which I could have well done without.

"Do you realise that you could have died Morgans," he said. "I've a good mind to put you on a charge."

I was hospitalised for a week. One minute I was burning up and the next minute I was freezing cold. Luckily for me there was little forward movement in the fighting and I was able to remain with my unit.

From Capua onwards we had to fight the Germans for every inch of land. The convoy of lorries continued moving along the road. I was allotted the duty of dispatch rider passing messages along the column. I had a BMW motorbike

Italy: July 1943 - May 1945
Badge of the 56th London Division
TRIESTE
MILAN
TURIN
VENICE
BOLOGNA
RAVENNA
GENOA
FLORENCE
The Gothic Line
NICE
CANNES
LEGHORN
ANCONA
PESCARA
ROME
R. Sangro
MONTE CASSINO
ANZIO
R. Volturno
R. Garigliano
NAPLES
SALERNO
BARI
TARANTO
SARDINIA
BRINDISI
MESSINA
PALERMO
SICILY
Mt Etna
CATANIA
AUGUSTA
SYRACUSE
MALTA

whose previous owner, a German dispatch rider, had been killed. It was dead of night with no lights permissible. Unfortunately for me one of the vehicles turned off the road in error. Collision was inevitable and the BMW and I parted company. The next morning I went to see the medical officer to have my cuts and abrasions cleaned up. He thought that I had cracked a couple of ribs and fitted a wide plaster around my torso. A week later it had to be removed, hairs and all. It was like being skinned and I wasn't even in battle.

The terrain was mountainous and the weather atrocious. Village after village fell, though they no longer resembled villages as they were flattened beyond recognition. We captured the village of Roccamonfina and then advanced towards Monte Cassino where we were bogged down for several weeks before eventually taking the mountain. We moved into the valley. Our comrades in arms during this terrible battle were the 8th Army Divisions, the 46th, 56th and 78th Divisions, the Gurkha Division, the Guards Brigade and later the 4th and 5th Indian Divisions, plus one American Division, the 88th. These divisions were represented as the 5th American Army.

The surrounding land was heavily mined and in the town of Cassino at the foot of the mountain the Germans were dug in. They had excavated the ground around the buildings and had driven Tiger Tanks down into the basements. The walls gave excellent protection as they were at least two or three feet thick. From ground level only the gun turrets were visible. This was to prove one of the worst battles of the War. I cannot relate the carnage and destruction I witnessed. The memories and nightmares are with me to this day.

The 56th Division moved northwards to cut the road and railway off so the Germans could not get further supplies to Cassino. My group advanced towards the Volturno river. Conditions were dreadful - wind, rain, and sludgy mud. The Volturno river captured, we continued to the Sangro river which we also captured. It took several months to get this whole area under our control.

The Rapido river was heavily defended and we were completely bogged down for several weeks. Once this river was breached, we pushed on to Garigliano into the Liri Valley. There our group was replaced by another division and we withdrew towards Capua where we rested. Replacement troops were brought in to make up for the heavy losses we had suffered. It was about this time General Montgomery left for Britain, we believed. Word passed around from an unreliable source that we, too, were about to embark for home. A few days later we returned to Naples, once again to board landing crafts.

Destination, Anzio.

At Anzio, the Germans were ready for us and were shelling the harbour to prevent us landing. Casualties were high even before we obtained a foothold on the beaches.

We got the Beach 'ead goin' with the Red Caps millin' round.
Rushed up the stores from off the ships and dumped 'em on the ground.
Then up an onto lorries - and so make room for more -
An' all the time the troops still came, a-pourin' on the shore.[1]

Landing achieved, we pushed on towards a little church, then to woodland near the coast, with continual bombardment all the way. Towards dusk we decided to remain in the wood. Shelling continued for about eight hours, through until dawn. We had a new recruit, only a young lad, and by morning he was a nervous wreck.

He was crying out, "Oh Mam, Oh Mam!"

"Morgans, go and get him and take him to the field hospital," the Captain said to me.

I never knew his name. There was no time for that kind of thing because we were constantly on the move. I hope they sent him home.

Daylight arrived and we advanced further up the coast from Anzio. Resistance was stiff and we dug in with our backs to the sea. The battleship Warsprite gave us cover, firing into the German lines.

Being from a mining family, my trenches were dug down at least six feet deep for cover. Even so, had it received a direct hit that would have been the end of me. I covered the top with earth and cloches of grass for camouflage whilst I was snuggled down inside. The Americans suffered casualties because their trenches were too shallow. If the landings proved difficult to hold they were ready to return to the ships, whilst we British held on by our teeth. We were even called `green horns' by some Americans and French Canadians, which did not endear them to the British lads, 8th Army veterans from the desert and France. Bombastic, big-headed, bragging so and so's they were. That's the way the lads felt about them.

For days we remained in our dug outs, battling against the Germans and the torrential rain. Bombardment continued day and night.

During this time my Warrant Officer gave me orders to carry dispatches from our position to the London Irish and London Scottish positions. The regular dispatch rider was ill.

"I am not a dispatch rider," I said, but I was chosen.

He gave me a mug full of black rum and said, "Off you go, Taff."

After imbibing the rum I feared nothing and no one. If I could make it along the road through the heavy shelling to the embankment I would be okay. I got on

---

1 Lt-Col H C Wheatley, OBETD late CO 45 Group, Royal Pioneers

my bike and let rip. Objective achieved, dispatches delivered, I set forth on the return journey to headquarters, fearless as ever on my BSA.

I earned the title "Mad Morgan" that day.

Our Division was so badly cut up that we were no longer regarded as an able fighting force. The Royal Berkshires were down to a handful of men as were the London Scottish and Irish. The middle-aged Commander of the Royal Berkshire Regiment sat down at the roadside and burst into tears.

"I've lost all my boys," he said.

It was very sad and upsetting rummaging through their uniforms for photographs of wives, children, mothers, fathers and sweethearts. There were letters from home and lucky charms. There was no time for personal, comforting letters from the commanding officers - only a brief statement in that dreaded telegram from the War Office. **Killed in Action**.

We, the remnants, were withdrawn from the lines and replaced by the American Rangers from the 5th Army. We pulled back, taking our ammunition with us. Four of our chaps were stacking ammunition when four German Tiger Tanks broke through our lines and one of their shells hit the ammunition dump. The four chaps took the brunt of the explosion and were blown to pieces. Their shoes remained - feet still in them. Finding no cover, I made myself small, expecting something to go right through me. My left ear was damaged and a small piece of shrapnel grazed my head. Luckily, my helmet took most of the impact.

I was transferred to a make-shift field hospital where I received treatment for my wounds. My pal came to see me and told me that our guns had destroyed the tanks. The next day a shell hit the hospital, killing some of the injured including two American nurses.

After my discharge from hospital I returned to what was left of our group. We remained in the area because we had to wait for replacement troops to arrive from Naples. Things began to go our way with regard to the continual fighting at Anzio and we advanced towards the Apennines Mountains. It was dead of winter and the roads were like glass which slowed down our advance into the Tiber Valley. Snow and ice bogged us down. Our feet and hands were frozen and our fingers had to work hard to pull rifle triggers.

We remained in this area for several months, eventually moving on and entering Rome on 5th June, 1944, the Germans having moved out in the early hours of the morning. There was no resistance and our group moved east of Rome to Tivoli.

A few days after the fall of Rome, King George VI visited us. We were ordered to shout, "Hip, hip hooray," three times as his car passed by.

Three weeks later we retreated towards Bari. Once again our Division suffered heavy losses and the Division had to be replenished with fresh troops. We were a full unit again, having been joined by the 1st Welch Regiment. We then proceeded up the Adriatic coastline to Pescara. By this time I had been transferred to the REME, the 168th London Infantry Brigade, LAD.

The battle continued through the mountains and along the coastal road to Ancona. New Zealanders were fighting along that road and we remained in the mountains with the 46th Division and the Indian Divisions. German resistance was very strong and our main objective was to make our way inland along the main road to Bologna. The 1st Welch Regiment were trapped and surrounded in a village and alas their fate was sealed. The London Scottish, however, managed to fight their way out of the village. The battle honours went to them that day.

From Bologna we made our way to Florence, fighting village by village. West of Arezzo we were involved in very heavy fighting in a village around the area of Montevarchi and the hills of Radda. It was dusk and we were moving by night to surprise the Germans by dawn. Unfortunately, two German planes came over the horizon and opened fire at our convoy. Several lorries were hit. One of our companies down in the valley had made camp for the night and was badly shot up. I was on the road and saw four Jocks trying to get into a pipe in the road for cover, each one pulling the other out as they tried to crawl inside. Suddenly I spotted a covered stone well. To avoid the bullets I lowered myself into the well, hanging on to the sides by my fingers, hoping I would not fall or get hit. The well was very deep and I realised that if I fell I would have been listed as **Missing in Action**. You see what lengths soldiers are prepared to go to in order to survive.

The planes left as darkness fell. We lost seventy men that day.

We moved on through the mountains and arrived at another village by dusk. My friend and I were in a fifteen hundred weight truck. The Germans shelled us as we tried to move along and we had to abandon the truck and jump into a ditch for cover but it was a jump from frying pan into fire. All around and under us were the German equivalent of hand grenades. `Tater mashers' we called them.

The next morning the village was captured and we drove the enemy out.

The Company then moved on towards Florence. On 18th June we managed to capture Assissi, then onwards to Ravenna. Several days later we arrived at the southern suburbs of Florence where we met opposition from German suicide squads and snipers left behind to delay our advance. With the aid of all divisions in the area, Florence was taken.

Our Infantry moved on but I and the others in the REME, LAD, twelve in number, remained in Florence. We took over a local garage in order to repair vehicles damaged in action. We saw no further military action in the War.

After a month in Florence we were transferred to Lake Como, a retreat resort for officers. Our job was to service and maintain motor boats used for their relaxation. After a few weeks here, orders were received stating that all members of 19 Group had to report to a transit camp in Milan. For the first time we were able to relax and enjoy ourselves, wandering around the city seeing the usual tourist sights. During the three weeks we stayed there a special show was arranged for us in a local theatre. Of course the nurses did not want anything to do with the ordinary squaddies and sat with the officers. We were up in the gods and some of the lads blew up `french letters' for devilment and parachuted them over the balcony to the stalls below. The ironic aftermath of that was that one chap later hung himself because he had contracted venereal disease and was too ashamed to go home.

You have to be brave to take your own life.

The time soon came for us to depart and we boarded a train bound for France via Switzerland. The carriages were locked and remained so throughout the journey, with no opportunity to alight. On arrival in France, I went from transit camp to REME workshop in Belgium and to yet another transit camp, in Dieppe.

24 - *Home Boys*

From Dieppe, orders came through for our repatriation to Britain and we boarded a ship bound for Newhaven. On landing at Newhaven, the propaganda leaflets dropped by the Germans throughout the campaigns abroad relating to the Yanks proved true. We noticed that they had monopolised our girls.

"What's wrong with us British lads?" the boys shouted.

But in spite of the money and provisions on offer from the Americans, the majority of our lasses remained faithful.

We boarded a train for Nottingham and stayed at Bulwell, main headquarters of the REME, for about a month, training and doing guard duties. It was decided to transfer me nearer to the Welsh borders and I was sent to Chester REME workshops where I repaired vehicles. As demobilisation approached I was transferred to Bridgend workshops.

Three weeks later I was ordered to make my way to Hereford for my demob.

The officer tried his best to persuade me to remain in the Army because good jobs would be available.

"After what I've been through?" I retorted. "No chance."

The day came and I was furnished with an ill-fitting suit, a reference stating that I was a qualified First Class motor mechanic and my fare home.

I arrived home to a street decorated for the End of War party. I walked through the front door to be greeted by Phyllis and my two children, Brian and Elaine. When I saw Elaine last she was three months old. Now she was three and a half.

"Elaine, this is your Daddy," Phyllis said.

My daughter replied, "Oh no it isn't. This is my Daddy," catching hold of her grandfather.

I was hurt at first but realised that she did not know me after all that time at war.

I tried for work in a local garage but the wage was too low to support a wife and two growing children so I returned to the colliery. A few weeks later I received a gratuity of seventy pounds for my War service and medals from the War Office: the 1939-1945 Star, the Africa Star, the Italian Star, the Defence Medal, the France and Germany Star and the 1939-1945 Service Medal.

Life returned to normal as I struggled to raise my family.

Was the sacrifice worth it?

The answer had to be yes at that particular time in world history, but now I am not so sure.

Since the War people have become both selfish and self-centred.

"So what!" they retort when I tell them about the men who gave their lives for freedom.

An old soldier I may be but it makes my blood boil. All those lovely boys who died for the likes of those ungrateful people. No. Dying for them was not worth it.

Memories flood back from time to time of my friends and comrades lying in foreign lands. Good, decent, honest chaps. Age comes thick and fast and many of us old soldiers have gone to greater glory above.

But it's like yesterday to me.

Some people say we should forget Remembrance Day because it glorifies war but they miss the point. It is not for the glory of war that we remember but out of respect to the memory of all who made the ultimate sacrifice.

They shall grow not old as we that are left grow old:
Age shall not weary them, nor the years condemn.
At the going down of the sun and in the morning
We will remember them.[1]

---

[1] Lawrence Binyon (1869-1943) *For the Fallen*, 1914.

25 - *Back in the Slow Lane*

The most traumatic years of my life were over and I had to re-adjust mentally to life in the slow lane. My thoughts were still embroiled in the arena of war and my memories were with all the friends that I had lost. Each night as I lay in my bed, I was re-living the nightmares of war. Sometimes I would wake up in a cold sweat, only to realise that I was safely tucked up in my bed. I was one of the lucky ones and I knew it. Phyllis always understood and made allowances for my diversity of moods. It wasn't going to be easy to settle down to a life of normality. A career in the motor trade was not to be and I had returned to the only work that was available. Mining. The comradeship of the war years was soon replaced by the another comradeship.

Owen was still Overman at Pengam Colliery and soon it felt as if nothing had really changed. I was one of the boys again. At work my mind was fully occupied. There was no time for reflection. There were too many dangers to let thoughts stray for long.

I did regret missing the earliest years of Brian and Elaine's childhood. Elaine found it hard to adjust to the fact that I was her father. She now had two fathers - Owen, whom she had accepted as her father during my absence, and her real father. Elaine insisted on calling both of us Dad, which caused some confusion at times. There were, however, no problems with Brian who was now nine years old.

Sarah Ellen's health had deteriorated during my absence. She had suffered her third stroke since the age of thirty six. Paralysed down one side, she was now bedridden and unable to speak properly. Phyllis was her nurse, companion and comforter, struggling to run the home, rear the children and look after the needs of the menfolk. Looking back, I now realise the pressure Phyllis was under. She was virtually a prisoner, leaving the house only to do the shopping. Even then she had to ask a neighbour to sit with Sarah Ellen and keep an eye on Elaine.

How Phyllis managed it all I will never know.

Sarah Ellen had gained a lot of weight because of inactivity and it was Phyllis who had to bathe her. The strain on Phyllis must have been tremendous but she never grumbled or moaned.

There were the usual crop of childhood illnesses such as measles and whooping cough. But when Brian contracted diphtheria he had a long spell in the isolation hospital at Aberbargoed. And I mean isolation. The hospital was situated on top of the mountain. Phyllis, with Elaine in the push chair, walked all the way from Cefn Fforest to Aberbargoed and back, just to have a glimpse of Brian through the hospital window. The hospital is long gone and Nature has reclaimed the land taken forcibly from her. Brian recovered, but the illness left a shakiness in his hand. But he could live with that.

At the age of four, Elaine fell down while playing and as all children do at such times ran to her mother to kiss and make it better. It turned out to be a relatively serious knee injury, resulting in many visits, over eleven years, to Mr Dilwyn Evans, Orthopaedic Specialist at Cardiff Royal Infirmary.

Gone was Owen's ambition to train Elaine for an athletic career.

The winter of 1947 was the worst that I had ever experienced. Naturally it was a delight for the children and an opportunity to get the sleigh out. For those of us who had to plough through it to get to work it was no picnic. Phyllis was in a very run down condition due to the effects of caring for her mother. An infection developed in Phyllis's right thumb which looked ghastly and she was referred to Cardiff Royal Infirmary. For seven weeks, Phyllis travelled in atrocious weather conditions to Cardiff, undergoing seven operations on her thumb. She had three pieces of bone removed with only a local anaesthetic and uttered not a sound. The Swedish specialist told her, "Mrs Morgan, you are one of the bravest patients that I have ever met!" and he shook her hand.

Phyllis resolved to keep her thumb, even though the specialist advised amputation in case of septicaemia. Phyllis should have been in hospital but there were no beds available because of the numbers of war wounded soldiers who had priority. According to the nurse, Phyllis was the first patient at the hospital to have penicillin.

The 5th July, 1948, was Phyllis's thirty fifth birthday and the day that marked the crowning achievement of my old friend and workmate, Aneurin Bevan. He had fought and campaigned for years for a health service free and available to all. And on that day the National Health Service came into being.

Aneurin would turn in his grave to see its demise.

Alas, Sarah Ellen never lived to enjoy the benefits. On 21st July, 1948, she passed away. God rest her soul. Owen, I believe, sensed that the end was near and had persuaded Phyllis to take the children to the local cinema, the Capital, at Blackwood. Phyllis was reluctant to go but gave in. Halfway through the film, a message was relayed to her that her mother had passed away.

She was heartbroken.

My immediate concern was for Phyllis. I knew only too well what torment and agony she was going through and I gave her all the support I could. The children were a great comfort to her and kept her busy most of the time.

Life has to go on and there was a home and family to look after. The days were not the problem, but night time was difficult. Sarah Ellen used to sleep downstairs in the front parlour and Phyllis could still hear her mother calling for her and would rush downstairs only to realise her mother was dead. This went on for several weeks, until Phyllis's nerves became very frayed. Doctor Richards suggested that we move house. It was the only solution and I began to search for somewhere suitable to our needs and our pocket.

Owen remarried. Although Phyllis took the children to visit him each week, we were no longer close.

We finally found a house in Gilfach, not too far from my work, close to the mining town of Bargoed. There were excellent shops and a very good bus service. It was an average mid-terrace property on the main road with front door opening directly onto the pavement. There were three rooms downstairs, front parlour middle room and kitchen with a cold tap. There was an outside flush lavatory. We had two bedrooms, the larger of which we converted into two rooms for Brian and Elaine. Elaine's school was within walking distance and Brian's was on the direct bus route, with the stop a yard or so from our front door.

We could be happy here. Legal transactions were completed and we looked forward to moving into our new home at 58 Park Place, Glifach.

Brian and Elaine were thrilled at the prospect of moving house. It was all a great adventure to them. With their grandmother being so ill, they could never invite their friends to play in the house or garden. For some reason, Elaine was under the impression that we were moving to the seaside and thought that Bargoed Colliery's hooter was the sound of ships in the harbour below. Poor Elaine, how disappointed she was when the truth was revealed to her.

At the weekends, I devoted my energy to home improvements. The two main requirements were a hot water system and a bath. With my knowledge of pipe fitting, I fitted a small hot water geyser over the kitchen sink and a bath in the far corner of the kitchen. There was no provision upstairs for a bathroom. I purchased an eight gallon geyser and fixed it over the bath.

Neither Phyllis nor I believed in hire purchase and we were prepared to wait until we had sufficient funds to make our purchases outright. It gave us great satisfaction to walk into a shop, cash in hand, and pay for an item. It was a wonderful sense of achievement to know that it was ours and no one could take it away. The mortgage was a different matter. Every Friday my pay packet was on the dining table. As long as I had my pocket money and the bills were paid, what

Phyllis did with the rest was no concern of mine. We had both lived through tough times and, like me, Phyllis knew only too well that every penny counted.

I was often surprised by Phyllis's thrift and what savings we had were put into a bank account which gave us a strong sense of security.

Phyllis was happy and derived great pleasure from getting her home together. The children settled in at their schools. Elaine went down with scarlet fever shortly after we moved, but fortunately soon bounced back.

When the miners' holidays arrived, as promised, I took the family on a caravan holiday to Ogmore-by-Sea. It was the best that I could afford at the time and in any case we relished the freedom of being in a caravan. The whole family was excited. It was the first of many holidays we were to have together and we thoroughly enjoyed ourselves.

The Forties were almost over and I sincerely hoped that the dark days of the war would never return. One of the main deprivations of the war on the home front, clothes rationing, ended on 15th March, 1949. Phyllis had once used a whole book of coupons to purchase a little red coat and leggings for Elaine. The country was still feeling the effects of war and until recovery was complete food and sweet rationing remained.

26 - *Don't Go Down the Mine, Son*

On 21st March, 1950, Brian celebrated his fourteenth birthday and would soon be leaving school. He was a good scholar, a real all-rounder, but more sports orientated than academically minded. The YMCA was a short distance away and he spent most of his leisure time playing football with the boys. At least Phyllis knew exactly where he was. Brian, or J B as the boys called him, was an excellent goalie and a very popular lad.

When the time came for Brian to leave school, I desperately tried to steer him away from mining. I wanted him to have an education and prospects.

Mining is a hazardous profession at the best of times. Each time I set foot in the cage, glancing skywards and taking a deep breath of fresh air, I wondered if this time would be my last. The cage was crowded with miners, our lives in the hands of the winder. The cage descended with speed down the pit shaft and when it eventually arrived at pit bottom your head was still at pit top, because the rate of descent gave the impression that you were ascending, not descending. It was a queer sensation. The air that greeted us was foul and smelled of rotten eggs.

Your eyes had to adjust to the dark and your lungs to the dusty conditions underground. Your lamp and helmet were the safety tools. There were no protective masks. Lunch box and jack in hand, you made your way to the face, not knowing what to expect when you arrived.

The mine could be anything from one mile deep to six hundred feet deep, with all those tons of earth above your head. Every creak and groan caused anxious moments, with the possibility of a roof fall and of being buried alive and entombed as some miners had been in the past. Fear was a constant companion. Reactions had to be swift. A split second decision could save your life when disaster struck. Often we worked on our sides or knees, alongside the constantly moving conveyor belt and other machinery which restricted avenues of escape. The greatest problem was the continual movement of the earth. You gained some space, only to lose it the next day.

It was a losing battle.

Pengam Colliery was as wet as ever. The water pumps were always submerged and repairs had to be done underwater. It was a good thing that I was a competent swimmer because I carried out the repairs. There I was in my birthday suit, submerging to lay the pipes in place to keep the pumps working, occasionally coming up for air only to descend again.

I served on the Mines Rescue Team for seven long years and I knew Man's vulnerability when pitted against Nature. As an ambulance man, my first concern was to save lives and to give speedy medical attention to those unfortunate miners who were injured. Some were beyond our help, like the boy crushed beneath a stone, his father helplessly looking on in a state of shock. It was hard not to have negative thoughts with the smell of death in your nostrils, but they had to be smothered because there was no place for them underground.

Very often potential disasters were caused by human error, especially fire, when a conveyor belt was inadvertently left running all night. The belt was made of rubber and friction caused smoke and heat subsequently resulting in fire. The rescue team would then be called out, kitted from head to toe with breathing apparatus, masks, protective clothing and fire fighting equipment. Miners' safety was our first priority and once we were satisfied that the area was cleared, the fire had to be tackled. The fire in the roadway would sometimes be like a thunderbolt and would build up momentum as it travelled along the coalface, with the added danger of pockets of gas adding fuel to the fire as it sped along. Our second priority was to starve the fire of oxygen, by sealing it off with whatever rubble was available and at hand, almost like a bricklayer sealing up a hole.

Gas was another possible cause of disaster and the two safety precautions used were the miner's friend, the canary, and the oil lamp. It was sad, but essential to the miner's safety to use the canary to test for gas in the atmosphere. Wearing breathing apparatus, we would gingerly carry the bird cage into the working face and if gas was present the canary would fall to the cage floor. There were two main gases to look out for, methane gas, which rises upwards, and black damp, which settles at the bottom of the roadway. The oil lamp measured the percentage of gas present at the coal face at the start of the shift. If there was two and a half percent of gas present, the men were evacuated from the face. Nine per cent of gas in the atmosphere was a warning that an explosion could be imminent. The flame was dark blue and when gas was present would elongate to establish the correct percentage. Methane gas rising to the surface would overcome a miner working on the roof supports, causing him to pass out and fall to the ground and possibly die if help was not at hand. Black damp, on the other hand, was completely airless and could catch you unawares if you did not have your wits about you. I myself experienced this hazard because for a few seconds I did not glance at the oil lamp, which had gone out. (An oil lamp does not burn in black damp). I became dizzy and realised in the nick of time.

Another tense and dangerous time underground was preparing the area for shot firing. So many things could go wrong and, as deputy, it was my job to prepare the explosives by placing them into waiting boring holes. Each of these explosives was numbered from 1 to 50 and had to be wired up individually to the main battery. I did this job alone. Some men offered to assist, but `Too many cooks spoil the broth'. It was my responsibility and by doing it myself I knew exactly what had and had not been done. Men's lives were at risk, including my own. I checked and double checked everything. I wound the battery box and raised the plunger, not before moving the men and myself two hundred yards back from the area. Each successive numbered explosive was fired by delayed action, the centre ones first (the keystone), the sides followed and then top and bottom in such a way as not to damage the supports, although such damage did inevitably occur. Clouds of dust were everywhere together with poisonous gases.

It was a never-ending battle to keep the coal face open. We struggled to place the roof supports in position, frantically trying to hold back the tonnage of earth above our heads. Sometimes we won, sometimes we lost and the whole coal face caved in before our eyes, burying the conveyor belt and coal-cutting machinery. It would take us six to seven weeks or even longer to establish another coal face. We were at war with the powerful forces of Nature which at times could be cruel and sometime kind. Nature was an adversary that we acknowledged and respected. Our lives depended on heeding the warnings and having our wits about us. I never thought that I would live to retire from the mines, having witnessed so many tragedies underground, but God has been good to me. I had always sensed that someone up there was watching over me.

The worthy beneficiaries of mechanisation would be the pit ponies whose days of slavery were numbered. Many a time, their sixth sense had saved their human companions from death. They would soon be able to enjoy fresh air and life in the fields. It would be goodbye to Justice, Kirk, Lion and Pride as they kicked off their shackles. We would remember them, and all their predecessors.

However, my immediate concern was to try to keep my son out of the mines.

27 - *Factory Work*

I was relieved when Brian decided to work at a local factory for the next few months, but he was not impressed. Once again, I tried to keep him out of the pit and I channelled him towards my personal love, motor vehicle maintenance. This worked for a while but his heart was not in it. Most of his friends had gone into the mining industry and Brian wanted to be with them. He was strong willed and determined to go his own way in life and he started work at Pengam Colliery. Hard as it was, Brian seemed to settle down to work in the mines. He never grumbled and did as he was instructed. He was proud when he received his first pay packet which gave him a feeling of independence. Three generations were now working at Pengam Colliery, Owen, myself and Brian. Owen's working life was coming to an end and when he left the mines his health was in tatters - the usual chest problems associated with the mining industry.

Elaine passed her 11 plus, only to be told a few days later that she could not go to Bargoed Grammar School because of an agreement between the counties of Monmouthshire and Glamorgan under which a percentage of pupils from Monmouthshire were allotted places in the Glamorgan Grammar schools and they had preference to a number of places at Bargoed Grammar School. We were very disappointed and so was Elaine's teacher, Miss Phillips. Elaine eventually made it to the Grammar School three years later, thanks to the headmistress of Bargoed Secondary Modern School, Miss Cowles.

The children had their pets, of course. There was a goldfish, Toby tortoise, Blackie our cat, Toby our Yorkshire terrier and, until he bit Elaine, a lively but tyrannical monkey. He ended his days in a monkey house owned by a private collector of primates in Cardiff. Encouraged by our friends, Doris and Charlie Pugh, the whole family became involved with cage birds. I can proudly say that some of my birds won First, Second and Third prizes over the years from the Cage Bird Society. It was a hobby that we all enjoyed and derived great pleasure from our canaries, finches and others - until a weasel destroyed the whole flock one night.

No more pets for the time being, we decided.

And indeed it was long time between. In 1957, we bought, Koo Chee of Elamor, a pekinese with an impressive pedigree, and re-named her Suzie. She cost fifteen guineas, half of which Elaine paid out of her pocket money and from the moment they met it was love at first sight. Suzie was jet black, with four cream socks, a v-shaped necklace, two cream eyebrows and a platinum blonde streak through her tail. Elaine was Suzie's mistress and trained her well.

There were many twists and turns in our lives in the Fifties. We applied to emigrate to Australia and were accepted, but when we learned that Brian would have to remain in Britain to do his National Service, we were not prepared to see our family split.

It was perhaps for the best. Brian had met Ann, his future wife, and she did not want to go to Australia. They planned to marry on 16th February, 1957. Elaine had finally got to Grammar School in 1956, but only months later had to go into hospital for a long-awaited operation on her leg. The specialist told us that if she did not have the operation she would be a cripple by the age of twenty. Elaine's stay in hospital coincided with Brian's marriage to Ann, on 16th February, and Elaine was very disappointed to miss the wedding.

On his marriage, Brian left Pengam Colliery and went to live in Aberbargoed, working at Bargoed Colliery.

Pengam Colliery was finally shut down as the water problem was getting out of control. I said goodbye to my workmates and got a job at Britannia Colliery.

Here I was afternoon deputy on a regular basis which was a considerable responsibility as you had to be alert at all times, especially with fifty men or so in your charge. The pressures were enormous and I was very irritable and would often lose my temper with the family over the slightest thing. They did not understand the pressures I was under and I did not understand the effect our quarrels were having on them.

It was only in later years that we understood each other better.

In 1960 Elaine sat her GCE Ordinary level examinations. After all her worrying she did not do too badly and decided to stay on at school. By June 1961 she had completed a two year Art course in one year and passed her Advanced level Art exam with a good grade. She was exhausted when she entered Barry Teacher Training College in the September. Phyllis and I were proud of her.

We were also proud to be grandparents. Alan came first, then Terry and last but not least, Anne.

My health was beginning to fail. I already had pneumoconiosis and the doctor found out that I had high blood pressure and angina, too. For some time, I plodded on like the old soldier I am, but eventually my mining days were over. I missed the companionship but can honestly say that I hated every day I worked in the mines.

I found work as a press operator in a car components factory, the `disabled factory' at Tir-y-Berth, especially for miners. I had thought my own health was bad but there were men there like fish out of water, gasping for every breath. Disabled as they were, they gave a full day's work.

At Christmas, there was a wonderful party laid on at company expense, with the lads providing the entertainment. The Welsh are famous for singing and we had the cream of singers among our workmates, regaling us with a medley of songs from the old days as well as current hits. Tommy Cross was the best singer, a Rhymney lad and a good tenor. He had a terrible stammer, yet he sang like an angel. There were comedians too, especially the older miners who had us rocking with laughter.

Elaine was anxious and unhappy at college. She confided in Phyllis who was like a sister as well as a mother to her. The stress was affecting Elaine's health and she decided not to continue. The principal did her best to persuade her to carry on, and so did I. But she was adamant and left college in June, 1963. I was extremely disappointed and refused to speak to Elaine for six weeks. Phyllis understood how Elaine felt and was a comfort to her. Phyllis made me realise that all that hard work since Grammar School had taken its toll on Elaine. She should have taken a year off before continuing with her education. Perhaps then things would have been different.

Elaine had a rest for a few months and then found a job as a dispatch clerk at a factory in Ystrad Mynach, about five miles away. The following year she applied for a job with the National Coal Board as a tracer at the Drawing Office of Penallta Colliery and was accepted, shortly before the entire office was transferred to Aberbargoed.

28 - *Moving House*

My biking days were long gone but thanks to Phyllis's thriftiness, our bank account was looking healthy and we were able to purchase a Mini Deluxe. It was sky blue. Now I did not have to wait in the cold for a bus to get to and from work. Phyllis was not too keen to get in the car because her nerve had gone since the motorbike accident of 1937 and she preferred to travel by bus or train. She had health problems and was suffering from rheumatoid arthritis which caused painful locking of her knees. She had recently had a chronic case of phlebitis in her legs and was immobile for six weeks. Elaine and I were concerned about the possibility of Phyllis falling down the stairs whilst we were at work and felt that a bungalow would be the best solution. At first Phyllis was not keen on the idea, being happy in the home she had lovingly built up over the years. Besides, she did not want to leave her friends and neighbours.

New bungalows were being erected on a site just below the famous Hengoed Viaduct near Ystrad Mynach. I bullied Phyllis into the car to go and see the site. It was in a very pleasant spot overlooking the valley and the Rhymney river to Maesycwmmer. We were both impressed with the location and I was able to choose the site on which the bungalow was already being built. Fortunately, we had enough money to pay for the bungalow outright as I hated being in debt. The bungalow was £2,800, including central heating. We made constant visits to the site during the following months to see how things were shaping up and there were inevitable delays due to a shortage of bricks. I thought we would never move in.

On St David's Day, 1st March, 1964, Phyllis's father Owen passed away. We attended the funeral to pay our last respects and to remember him as he was before his remarriage. That was the last time we set foot in 24 Davies Street, Cefn Fforest.

The last link in the family chain had been severed forever.

Months passed and still the bungalow had not been completed, although we had hoped to be in by Christmas. Neither had the estate agent found a purchaser for our house, so we decided to look for a prospective buyer ourselves. We were successful within a month and although the buyer was prepared to wait, he and his family did want to move in by Christmas. Even though our bungalow was not quite ready, we moved in on 16th December. The hall and lounge woodblock floors had just been varnished and we had to walk on strategically placed planks to allow the floors to dry out. In spite of roughing it for a couple of days, we managed to enjoy Christmas in our new home.

The road was not yet built and we were marooned in a sea of mud. The car looked as if it had been in a mountain rally. When Phyllis went to the village to do her shopping she had to carry spare shoes to change at the end of the lane and put the muddy ones in a plastic bag until she re-negotiated the mud on her return.

Only four bungalows were completed when we moved in and our neighbours were young couples, both working and out all day. Phyllis was isolated and unhappy and it took months for her to get used to the move.

I worked hard to get the garden into shape, laying paths and boundaries and digging out a huge tree trunk where the front lawn was going to be. Elaine was a good help, clearing debris with a wheelbarrow.

In April, 1965 Elaine's penfriend, Gunhild, arrived unexpectedly from Denmark. She was impressed with the hilly landscape because Denmark is so flat but she was unimpressed by the First and Second Class railway carriage system because in Denmark everybody, rich or poor, used the same carriage and paid the same price. The following June, Elaine made a return visit and spent a week at the University and a week on Gunhild's parents' farm on the island of Lolland. The boat and train trip, including a cabin on board, cost £36.00 return, vastly different from today's prices. Elaine was impressed when she met a ten year old girl who could speak English, French and German as well as her native language. It madc Elaine feel ashamed of her own lack of languages.

I had decided to change cars and traded in the mini for an A40, thinking that Phyllis would be happier with a bigger car. She was not, so it was used for work.

My working life in the factory turned out to be the happiest days of my life. The lads were a grand bunch, always laughing and joking even when they felt below par. However, there were times when I dreaded Monday mornings and would be shocked to hear that someone I had been talking to on Friday had died during the weekend. In one year we lost thirty four workmates from the industrial disease pneumoconiosis. That was the price a miner had to pay for making profits for the coal owners.

Phyllis and I both still wished that Brian was not working in the mines. There were problems in the South Wales Coalfields, with occasional strikes and the early years of Brian's marriage were sometimes difficult as a result. His wife, Ann, had heart problems - leaking heart valves - and was to undergo surgery three times. Ann's father and mother, Jim and Lou, were a great support to them. The highlight of our week was when Brian brought the children to visit.

The miners themselves were not the only ones to pay a high price. I have lived through many mining disasters but the tragedy of 21st October, 1966 is etched on my mind as a day I will never forget and nor will anyone in the Welsh mining valleys. I had lived in fear of death and destruction below ground but never thought it could happen on the surface. The coal tips on the surrounding mountains were an eyesore that every mining community put up with, but with the inclement weather and ravages of time the waste material became more menacing day by day. High above the school in the village of Aberfan in Mid Glamorgan, coal waste - now slurry and sludge - was beginning to slither and slide down the mountainside, like lava from a volcano but swifter and more deadly. Without warning, it engulfed the school and buildings directly in its path. One hundred and forty four were killed, one hundred and sixteen of them children. A whole generation wiped out. My heart went out to all those families.

The National Coal Board was once again re-organising and the work in Elaine's office was slack. She was bored and the following July joined the Civil Service and was working about five miles from home. She was keen to learn to drive and the greatest mistake I made was to try and teach her myself. I will spare you the details of me shouting, "Go on. There's plenty of time," and the smash that followed. Suffice to say that Elaine quite rightly vowed never to listen to me again. She is a competent driver today, but not thanks to me.

My own life was hard and I must be honest I was very much down on Elaine, with an almost Victorian attitude. I frequently and needlessly was too much of a disciplinarian. It was this that caused her to leave home for a year. The fault was mine. I did not give her credit for using her own judgement.

Elaine found digs in Cardiff which was easily accessible to the bus service for Caerphilly where she worked. She did not want to go and was unhappy and lonely there, but there was no way she would come back on her own initiative. She was a chip off the old block. At weekends she would come home to see her mother and Brian, who visited every Sunday.

I was very glad when we were reconciled and Elaine came home.

The British Motor Company had now been taken over by British Leyland which made us feel insecure at the time but we need not have worried. We were treated fairly and I was offered a press tool maintenance job which suited me well.

Sometimes the work involved tool making and if I felt that a tool could be improved upon I would drop my suggestion in the box provided. Anything to help. Reward was the last thing on my mind. The Prime Minister, Mr Edward Heath, visited our factory on one occasion and those who loved the limelight crowded round for the photo-call, but not me.

I was surprised and pleased to be selected, in 1970, to be part of a group which would visit a factory in Belgium for a week - all expenses paid. There and on our visit to Holland we received a wonderful welcome. At Seneffe we were shown around the factory where we found that the men were ex-coal miners like ourselves.

29 - *Rocky Mountains*

The major political, social and economic events of these decades were of great interest to me and it is not because of lack of awareness or lack of emotional involvement that I do not comment here on wars, assassinations, explorations, investiture, deaths and births. These matters are well documented elsewhere. Perhaps suffice to say that my feelings are always with the common folk who struggle to survive, whether they are in Wales, Vietnam, Northern Ireland, or elsewhere in these islands and across the world.

Some changes become harder than others to get to grips with. I could cope with decimalisation of the currency in 1971, although the metric system is not for me and I still think in yards, feet and inches, stones, pounds and ounces.

But there was not a great deal I could do about my failing health. I carried on until one day I collapsed over the work bench. I would not give up work, although Phyllis pleaded with me. I continued working for two more years.

In 1973 I had a second collapse and my doctor confronted me.

"Do you want to live longer, Mr Morgan?" he asked.

"Yes, doctor."

"Then give up work now."

On his advice, at the age of sixty two, I became a gentleman of leisure.

Having worked since the age of fourteen I found it very hard to adjust to retirement. What was I going to do with all this time on my hands? There was plenty of work to do in the garden during the summer months but winter robbed me of that pleasure. Phyllis was happy to have me at home for company. Her rheumatoid arthritis was getting progressively worse and I was to prove a good help around the bungalow. I could cook, sew, iron and turn my hand to most jobs around the house and it was now my turn to repay Phyllis for looking after me and the children.

I had mellowed over the years although we had our stormy moments in the past. I will never forget the day when Phyllis and I had a row and in my temper I knocked the cup of tea against the wall. Diplomatic as ever, Phyllis said, "That was a silly thing to do. You have just finished papering the room. Now you will have to do it again. It's my turn to break the crockery now," she said. "I'll break the cup, you break the saucer, then the plate, then the jug."

It was so funny that I just sat down and burst out laughing and thought to myself, "Good for you." Phyllis cured me, although I still lost my temper on occasions.

Our dog, Georgie, was happy with both of us at home. She was loyal, affectionate, comical and a good house dog. She was also an excellent traveller and on two occasions we drove to Cornwall and Dorset for caravan holidays. Brian came to spend a few days with us.

In August, 1973, Elaine fulfilled an ambition that she had carried with her since the age of six. She used to spend hours poring over a set of Encyclopedia Phyllis and I bought, *Pictorial Knowledge*. She loved the sections on foreign countries and was impressed by a colour picture of Mount Robson in the Canadian Rockies. At the age of thirty one, Elaine achieved her ambition. On a holiday of a lifetime the pages from that book came alive for Elaine as she gazed at Mount Robson from the Canadian highway in the heart of the Rockies.

In the last year of this decade there was a birth and a death in my family. On 2nd June, 1979, our first great-grandchild, Alan, was born. We were so proud, as were Jim and Louise, Ann's parents.

In the following November my father passed away. I am glad that I made peace with him on my last visit to the Forest. It is wrong not to forgive and forget. His last wish was to be buried at St John's Church, Cinderford where most of his family were interred. My only regret is that in death Mam and Dad are still apart, he in Cinderford and Mam and my brothers in Bedwellty.

May they find reconciliation in death.

30 - *Russia and Spain*

An upsurge of tension between East and West marked the start of 1980, with the shooting down of a passenger airline which had strayed into Soviet territory. All were lost and there was condemnation and recriminations. Our planned visit to the Soviet Union looked uncertain.

Elaine wanted Phyllis and myself to go on holiday together while she remained at home, but we both relied on Elaine to handle the holiday arrangements and felt more secure in her company. The decision was that at the beginning of July Elaine and I would go to the Soviet Union and Phyllis would stay at home and look after Georgie, who was twelve years old and had never been in kennels. Phyllis would then go on holiday with Elaine to Spain in September.

Over the years there had been so much propaganda about the Soviet Union that I looked forward to seeing for myself. Our trip involved seven flights from Moscow to Khabarovsk in the Soviet Far East, visiting the Siberian towns of Irkutsk and Bratsk. We stood on the shores of the largest landlocked freshwater lake in the world, Lake Baikal, before returning to Leningrad - now once again St Petersburg - our favourite city. Language was the main barrier but Elaine had learned enough Russian to understand signs and to ask directions. The people were no different to us and had a sense of humour. My impression at the time was that they were like the people of Britain in the 1930s. Elaine said that she felt safer on the streets here than when she had crossed into America during her Canadian trip. I had long wished to visit the USSR and this ambition had now been fulfilled.

Phyllis loved the sun and the Spanish people and was confident with Elaine at her side. They visited Ronda, Seville and Granada, the latter they fell in love with, especially the sunlit view from the Alhambra with snowcapped mountains behind.

I think there was Spanish blood in Phyllis. She was slow to lose her temper but when she did you certainly knew it.

Late evening on 9th February, Elaine was rushed into hospital thanks to the swift action of Doctor Owen Thomas. We did not know how close to death she

was. Brian took us to the hospital the following morning and the specialist, Mr John Roberts, called us into the room and said,
"I am sorry to tell you that Elaine is not coming back. Go home and prepare for the worst."

We were numb with shock. I was seventy and Phyllis sixty eight. It was earth shattering for us.

"Elaine has pancreatitis and her whole system has been poisoned. She is being transferred to Cardiff Royal Infirmary today," said Mr Roberts.

How Brian drove us home that day I will never know. We sat down and cried in each other's arms.

Elaine's kidneys failed and she was rushed into intensive care and put on a ventilator. The prognosis was not good. The next six weeks were a nightmare for Brian, Phyllis and me. Elaine was in a twilight zone, hovering between life and death, unconscious and unaware of the drama going on around her. Phyllis spent a fortnight at the hospital in a special unit provided for this kind of emergency and during the course of those weeks Elaine's heart stopped four times. She even missed her thirty ninth birthday and was unable to see the cards from family, friends and colleagues that were placed around her bed. She had undergone two operations, a tracheotomy and an exploratory operation. At the end of six weeks, the doctor decided to switch off the ventilator and for a few minutes we all sat on a knife's edge.

It was touch and go.

The doctor said, "I'm not sure, but I think we've got her. Yes we have."

Elaine started breathing for herself. It was a terrific belated birthday present for us all. Mr Mike Harne and his wonderful team had pulled Elaine through and we could not thank them enough for all their devoted skill and attention.

"We didn't do it all, Mr Morgan, Elaine's a good little fighter too," said Mr Harne. "Your daughter has been to hell and back and she still has a long way to go."

For the second time in her life, the wonderful staff at that great hospital, Cardiff Royal Infirmary, had saved our daughter's life.

In March, Elaine was transferred back to Llandough Hospital, still seriously ill but out of immediate danger. Phyllis and I had to catch three separate buses to get to the hospital because Brian was at work all day and could not take us down until late evening. It was a struggle, but we were determined to be with her.

There were still times of despair because we could see no signs of improvement and we sat down in silence and just stared at each other. Phyllis was stronger than me during this time of stress. Elaine underwent a further operation in April, performed by Mr John Roberts. The gall bladder - the culprit that caused the pancreatitis - was removed, as was her spleen and appendix and a by-pass was made from her stomach to her intestine. Unable to keep food and drink down, she was extremely weak, with very low blood pressure. Occasionally when she sat up she would pass out and once her heart stopped.

We sat by her side seven days a week for four and a half months. There was no life in her at all. One day I left the hospital in tears when Elaine said to me, "Dad, if they tell you that I am going to die, please take me home."

During the last month in hospital, we began to see signs of improvement, although the vomiting persisted for several years. If she had not been fed intravenously, she would have starved to death. I had a gut feeling that Elaine would improve better at home, even though she could hardly walk and I approached the doctors and made that suggestion.

"Her blood pressure is still low and she isn't really fit enough to go home," I was told.

After conferring, they decided to give it a try. My observation was right. The home environment did the trick, although she had to travel every week to the hospital by ambulance for check ups. It was great to have her home again. It was mid June and Elaine was virtually a prisoner at home apart from the hospital visits. It was nearly two years before she took her first walk to the village in the week before Christmas, 1982. From the moment Elaine was discharged from hospital, Phyllis's health was affected as a result of those traumatic months in 1981, but she was determined not to let her daughter down. Her child came first.

Elaine retired from work because of her illness. Having watched how she suffered during that illness, I was determined that she would not work again, not that she was well enough anyway. Her friends Heather, Margaret and Haulwen rallied round and were a great support throughout that terrible experience.

Throughout 1983, Elaine was still attending Out-patients at the University of Wales Hospital for check ups.

Trouble was brewing in the South Wales Coalfield during the course of the year, and miners were afraid of losing their jobs through pit closures. Mistrusting the government's assurances, the miners decided on strike action in March, 1984. They were fighting for their livelihoods, wanting work not the dole queue. We gave Brian all the help we could in that terrible year and backed the miners' struggle to the hilt.

The Foresters supported the miners' efforts to save their jobs because they remembered the demise of their own coal mining industry only too well. Graham Morgan, my nephew, organised transportation of food supplies for South Wales miners and their families, which had been generously donated by the people of Cinderford and surrounding areas. He and his friends ran the gauntlet of police road blocks to deliver sorely needed food supplies to the South Wales Miners' Headquarters at Tonypandy in the Rhondda Valley. The Foresters' kindness has not been forgotten. I was proud of Graham , and so were Kath and Merlin.

The struggle was lost and within a few years twenty eight mines in the South Wales valleys were closed, including Tower Colliery. Today, due to the miners' determination, that colliery is open again - under miners' ownership.

On 22nd April, 1985, Phyllis and I celebrated our Golden Wedding. I could not believe how the years had flown. Ours was not a perfect marriage, very few are. We had our ups and downs like any other couple but were still together for all that. Fifty years earlier we had exchanged our vows, to love, honour and obey, in sickness and in health, until death us do part. We kept those vows as God intended. A marriage has to be a team effort and if the partners do not pull together and resolve their differences it cannot succeed. I am happy to say, ours did. Brian and Elaine wanted to take us out for a special meal to celebrate but I disliked being in the limelight and being fussed over and Phyllis and I decided it would be a quiet affair, at home. Elaine did us proud and the spread was as good as anything that could be served up in a restaurant, but she left the Celebration Cake to the professionals. It was beautiful and decorated with all the trimmings required for a Golden Wedding. There were flowers and other gifts that are highly treasured to this day. Elaine said, "When it comes to your Diamond Wedding, Dad, you will have to have a real celebration."

Elaine was a great help to us, even though that terrible illness had drained her stamina and affected her health. With Phyllis's health in steady decline, Elaine was determined to care for her mother, whom she adored. Like her mother, she was a caring, loving and dutiful daughter. She still is and I am proud of her, Brian too. I am so glad that both of them have their mother's ways and temperament.

We did manage to take Phyllis on holidays during the next few years and she enjoyed them, even though her walking ability was limited. However, she refused to sit in a wheel chair. Her movements were slow and painful yet she refused to give in.

On the very last holiday in Western-super-Mare, Phyllis spent most of her time within the confines of the hotel and Elaine and I knew that Phyllis would not be able to cope with any more holidays. Yet she never once complained about being housebound. It was very sad to see such an active person confined to the boundaries of her home. Yet Phyllis was still young at heart and young in her mind. One of my fondest memories was of Phyllis sitting in her chair listening to music on the wireless, her foot tapping to the tempo. She loved music, especially when doing the housework. Jokingly Elaine would say, "When you die, Mam, I am going to put a sweeping brush and a radio in your coffin and a hammer and chisel in Dad's."

We had a good laugh over that.

By 1988 we were great-grandparents nine times over: seven boys and two girls. Alan's children: Alan junior, Nikki and Zoe; Terry and Trudi's children: Wayne, Helen and Craig; and Anne and Paul's children: Lee, Paul junior and Neil.

31 - *Goodbye, Phyllis*

It was 24th February, 1990, Elaine's forty eighth birthday and with the month almost over we looked forward to the light nights. We are summer people and hate winter, enjoying the first flush of spring flowers in the garden. There was plenty of work for me out there. I was the vegetable man, still gardening the way my grandfather in the Forest of Dean taught me. Elaine was the flower girl - like her Dad, a Child of the Forest. She watched me like a hawk as she would spend pounds on flowers only to see them turfed out as weeds when I tidied up the borders.

The years pass so quickly when you reach my age. Too quickly. Phyllis was losing confidence in walking and was now using a zimmer and was finding it extremely difficult to get out of the chair. Yet she was very strong willed and would not give in. She was suffering but never complained.

The armchair she bought the previous Christmas was a great comfort to her and she would fall asleep quite easily. Elaine and I tried not to disturb her and would get on with some gardening if the weather was good.

Phyllis was finding things difficult and we stayed close in case she fell. She still wanted to do things for herself if she could.

"I'm not half the woman Mam is," Elaine said. "I wish I had her strength."

"You are your mother's daughter, Elaine, made from the same mould," I replied.

I firmly believe, and so does Elaine, that Phyllis realised that something was going to happen to her. One day while they were chatting, Phyllis said to Elaine, "You'll have a lot of clothes after me love!"

"I don't want your clothes, Mam, I want you," Elaine replied.

Phyllis looked into Elaine's face and gave a lovely smile.

It was Sunday, 1st July, a real summer's day with warm sunshine permeating through the window and brightening the whole room. Phyllis loved the sunshine and was sitting in her chair, the sun warming her face. Elaine and I were preparing the Sunday dinner, as usual, while Phyllis settled back to listen to her favourite programme, Desmond Carrington's *All Time Greats*.

Elaine decided to spend a pleasant hour in the garden, sitting under the trees by the pond. She asked Phyllis if she wanted her to stay with her, but unselfish as ever, Phyllis said, "It's alright, love."

Elaine settled Phyllis in the chair and put the television on for her. Tea time came around and Elaine prepared some sandwiches for Phyllis and carried them in on a tray.

Phyllis said, "That was quick."

"There's a good film on, Mam, that will suit us both. Julie Andrews and Richard Harris," she said.

I watched the Sunday sport in the bedroom and the two women settled down to watch the film. There is a scene in the film where Julie Andrews is giving birth and gives a blood curdling scream. Elaine glanced towards Phyllis who had just taken her glasses off and before she could put her hand to her side, Phyllis started to shake. Elaine leapt out of the chair, ran to the phone and shouted to me, "Dad, something is wrong with Mam. I'm calling the ambulance."

I rushed to Phyllis's side and she whispered, "Reg, Reg."

They were the last words she spoke.

Within five minutes the paramedics arrived and while those wonderful people were attending to Phyllis, Elaine called Brian who came down immediately. Elaine accompanied her mother in the ambulance while Brian and I followed in the car to the Prince Charles Hospital, Merthyr Tydfil. When we arrived in Casualty, the doctor called us in. Phyllis was still conscious and able to hear. The doctor was brisk and to the point.

"It's a hard stroke and she is not going to make it," he said.

I know that Phyllis heard what was said and knowing her strength of character and willpower, she fought tooth and nail for the next few days, but the odds were against her. Elaine never left her side the first night, but Brian ordered her home the next day because she was worn out from lack of sleep.

"You have to keep your strength up for Dad. There is nothing you can do. Mam is in good hands," Brian said.

During the early hours of 5th July, Brian received a telephone call to say that Phyllis was deteriorating and could we come immediately. The hospital was some distance away and we raced there. But by the time we arrived it was too late. Our lovely Phyllis had slipped away.

It was her seventy seventh birthday. Elaine, with birthday cards in hand, kissed Phyllis and said, "Happy birthday, Mam," followed by Brian and then myself. Apparently as I kissed Phyllis on the forehead, Brian and Elaine heard breathing and a heavy sigh in the room. They looked at each other but said nothing. I did not hear this because my hearing is impaired. There were tears and the nurse said gently to Elaine, "It's selfish to cry for ourselves. You must think of your mother who was suffering."

Elaine was not only crying for the loss of her mother but for the fact that Phyllis had died alone.

"It's awful to die alone, Dad. I so much wanted to be at Mam's side."

For the first and only time in her life Elaine envied those who were given that opportunity to be there at the end. Now she understood how her mother must have felt when Sarah Ellen passed away.

Phyllis, my dear wife and mother of my two wonderful children, was at rest and free from pain and suffering. I realised that Phyllis's passing was a blessed relief. There was no way Brian, Elaine and I would have wanted Phyllis to be like a cabbage for the rest of her life because she herself would have hated that too. God was good to Phyllis. He always works in mysterious ways and knew what was best for all of us. At times like this we fail to understand His methods or purpose, but ours not to wonder why.

Phyllis was laid to rest in Bedwellty Cemetery, not far from where Brian lives. Although I am still a Forester at heart, when my turn comes, I too will be laid to rest, united for all eternity with the woman I loved and lost.

God Bless you, Phyllis.

The fifth of July we will never forget,
The day of your birth,
The day of your death.
Precious memories of you, Dear Mam
All the years through
Our thoughts and our wishes
Are always with you.
God Bless you Mam.
Flowers fade, memories never.

The rock on which our house was built was splintered, but not shattered. The foundation remained solid. Phyllis was the rock on which it stood, just as Simon Peter was the rock on which God built the Christian Church. Her faith was strong, as was her strength of character and will and she would not wish us to grieve, but to show courage and go forward in life.

Phyllis was the most unselfish person I had ever met, a characteristic which she passed to both her children. She was everything a wife and mother should be: loyal, faithful and steadfast in everything she did, caring, loving and devoted to her children whom she adored - and as honest as the day. It was going to be difficult without her because she had been part of our lives for so long. We had been partners for just over fifty five years and we had taken the rough with the smooth, the lean years with the plenty and yet we had stuck together.

God! I was going to miss her.

After losing a loved one it is strange how you begin to reproach yourself. Did I do the right thing by her? Was I a good husband? I felt a strong sense of guilt as I expressed my innermost thoughts to Elaine.

"You were a good husband. You always put your money on the table. The only thing, Dad, was your temper, which you lost often, but you meant no harm," Elaine said.

I had to admit that she was right.

"You have mellowed in your old age and things have been good. Don't reproach yourself. You were good to Mam and did everything you possibly could. We all have faults, we're not perfect, any of us," she said.

Elaine had expressed that she too had misgivings, whether she had done the right thing.

"If we had called the doctor against Mam's wishes, Dad, maybe things would have been better and Mam would have been alive today," she said.

I think all that self-reproach is part of the grieving process. If only this. If only that.

Elaine's friend Haulwen was a great help and comfort throughout the following months, as were Heather and Margaret and all our friends. Haulwen still came to tea on Thursdays, but it was never the same again. Someone wasn't with us any more.

We both had to come to terms with life without Phyllis and the bond between Elaine and I strengthened with each passing day. We were like a pair of crutches supporting each other through the `down days'. Elaine grieved inwardly as I did. The quiet moments were the worst and we tried to avoid those moments by keeping ourselves busy around the home, doing everything not to think and reflect. The night times were worst of all and very often I would hear Elaine crying alone in her bed. Yet she never betrayed her feelings in public. Christmas would never be the same again. As our first Christmas without Phyllis approached, we wished it would never come. It was the very first special event without her. It was now six months since Phyllis's passing and Elaine had borne her mother's death well, but come Christmas the delayed reaction of shock struck with vengeance. Elaine just could not understand what was wrong. There was deep anger inside her and being a gentle person it was totally alien to her nature. Her nerves took a real pounding and I was worried about her. I knew that I had to be strong for both of us. Life had made me a little tougher, able to take the blows, but not Elaine.

"I feel so sorry for you, Dad, you've lost Mam too. I feel so guilty," she said.

"Never mind love, you've got me and we'll get through this together," I replied.

We spent the first Christmas alone. Although Brian and Ann asked us to spend Christmas Day with the family, we wanted to be alone at that time and our thoughts were of the last Christmas we had spent together as a family.

The days became months, the months became years and gradually we began to see a light at the end of the tunnel, although the pain of parting is still with us. Elaine and I have become inseparable and the bond between us has strengthened. It is comforting to know that we are there for each other in times of despair. It has been hell, but I know that Phyllis is proud of our courage to come to terms with her loss and I know she will be happy to see how close we have become as a father and daughter should be.

Wherever you are Phyllis, I promise that I will continue to do my duty towards our family until the day on which I will be re-united with you in death. I made my vows on the 22nd of April, 1935 and even though death has kept us apart these last few years, I solemnly swear that I will not fail the two wonderful children you have left in my keeping.

God Bless you Phyllis, until we meet again.

EPILOGUE

On 16th April 1995 I was eighty four years old. Would I live my life again, you ask. For my family, yes. But I can honestly say that one life time is enough for any man. Life has been far from easy, but I have survived. Something inside me would not let go.

But we also rejoice in our sufferings, because we know
that suffering produces perseverance; perseverance character;
and character, hope.
And hope does not disappoint us.
Romans 5, v2.

Hope of a better life has been the driving force in my life. You are still learning until the day of your death. I have no wish to die but I am not afraid.

The time and choosing is God's alone, but I live in hope.